ON YOUR HONOUR

ON YOUR HONOUR

By Roger Leach and Colin Wakefield

JOSEF WEINBERGER PLAYS

LONDON

ON YOUR HONOUR
First published in 2008
by Josef Weinberger Ltd
12-14 Mortimer Street, London, W1T 3JJ
www.josef-weinberger.com
general.info@jwmail.co.uk

Copyright © 2008 by Roger Leach and Colin Wakefield
Copyright © 1998 by Roger Leach and Colin Wakefield as an unpublished dramatic composition

Reprinted 2010

The authors have asserted their moral right to be identified as the authors of the work.

ISBN   987 0 85676 315 1

This play is protected by Copyright. According to Copyright Law, no public performance or reading of a protected play or part of that play may be given without prior authorisation from Josef Weinberger Plays, as agent for the Copyright Owners.

From time to time it is necessary to restrict or even withdraw the rights of certain plays. **It is therefore essential to check with us before making a commitment to produce a play.**

NO PERFORMANCE MAY BE GIVEN WITHOUT A LICENCE

AMATEUR PRODUCTIONS

Royalties are due at least one calendar month prior to the first performance. A royalty quotation will be issued upon receipt of the following details:

Name of Licensee
Play Title
Place of Performance
Dates and Number of Performances
Audience Capacity
Ticket Prices

PROFESSIONAL PRODUCTIONS

It is important to check with us before committing yourself to a professional production since Josef Weinberger Ltd does not in every case control all aspects of professional rights.

OVERSEAS PRODUCTIONS

Applications for productions overseas should be addressed to our local authorised agents. Further details are listed in our catalogue of plays, published every two years, or available from Josef Weinberger Plays at the address above.

CONDITIONS OF SALE

This book is sold subject to the condition that it shall not by way of trade or otherwise be resold, hired out, circulated or distributed without prior consent of the Publisher. **Reproduction of the text either in whole or part and by any means is strictly forbidden.**

Printed in England by Good News Press, Ongar, Essex

ON YOUR HONOUR was first presented by Double Honours Productions in association with Theatre Maketa at the Jermyn Street Theatre, London, on 11th September 2007. The cast was as follows:

CHRISTIAN	Greg Gillespie
NICK WILLMOTT, QC	Philip Childs
TONI TAYLOR	Luciana Lawlor
HUGO BARNES, QC	Alister Cameron
GERALD BLUNT	Edward Fulton
HILARY WILLMOTT	Janet Rawson
SIR HARRY LUMSDEN-CLARK	Stan Pretty
LIZ LUMSDEN-CLARK	Leda Hodgson

Directed by Colin Wakefield
Designed by Colin Mayes
Lighting and Sound by Luci
Company Stage Manager Peter Adshead
Assistant Stage Manager Ryan Burkwood

CAST OF CHARACTERS

Hugo Barnes, QC (51)

Nick Willmott, QC (51)

Hilary Willmott (Nick's wife) (42)

Liz Lumsden-Clark (Hilary's sister), a Circuit Judge (44)

Sir Harry Lumsden-Clark (Hilary and Liz's father), the new Lord Chancellor (66)

Gerald Blunt (a civil servant) (25)

Toni Taylor, a solicitors' secretary (20)

Christian, a student (19)

The action takes place one Saturday afternoon and evening in a luxury bedroom at the Harcourt Hotel, Birmingham.
Time: The Present

ACT ONE

Scene One	Saturday 1.00 PM
Scene Two	Saturday 6.00 PM

ACT TWO

Scene One	Saturday 8.00 PM
Scene Two	Ten minutes later

ROGER LEACH

Roger was born in Australia and read English at Sydney University before training as an actor at the Central School of Speech and Drama in London. He worked in England for the rest of his life, and was probably best known as Sgt. Penny in *The Bill*, a part he played for six years. He was also a highly successful stage actor, whose leading roles included Lambert Le Roux in *Pravda*, Scrooge in *A Christmas Carol*, Subtle in *The Alchemist* and Bluntschli in *Arms and the Man*. He also starred in musicals, including Peachum in *The Threepenny Opera* and Doolittle in *My Fair Lady*. For 18 years he toured with actor and musician Michael Lunts in a two-man show of their own devising called *Quirkish Delight*. With Colin Wakefield he wrote two stage comedies, *Double or Twin* and *On Your Honour* along with the thriller *Audience with Murder*.

COLIN WAKEFIELD

Colin is a former law lecturer, and he trained as an actor at the Webber Douglas Academy. Acting roles include Victor in *Private Lives*, Lloyd in *Noises Off*, the tile role in *The Mikado*, Judge Turpin in *Sweeney Todd* and Bottom in *A Midsummer Night's Dream* for the award-winning company Cheek by Jowl. TV and film work includes *Extras, Silent Witness, State of Play, The Rector's Wife, Vanity Fair* and Peter Knox QC in the Sky TV reconstruction of *The Hutton Inquiry*. As well as his work with Roger Leach, Colin has written a thriller with David Gillespie called *Sleep No More*. With composer Kate Edgar he wrote eight traditional pantomimes for Salisbury Playhouse and three actor/musician family musicals for Winchester Theatre Royal, produced by Ian Liston's Hiss and Boo Company. Nine of these shows have been published by Josef Weinberger Ltd. Kate and Colin have also written four musicals commissioned and performed by schools and youth groups, including *Witchwood*, an environmental piece for up to 300 students. Colin has recently completed *My Dear Howey,* a one-woman show for Pauline Gray based on the letters of Georgiana, First Countess Spencer of Althorp, and he is currently writing *A History of England* in rhyming iambic pentameter, which (at a projected 30,000 lines) will be the longest poem in the English language.

ACT ONE

Scene One

Saturday 1.00 PM.

A very smart bedroom in the Harcourt Hotel, Birmingham. The hotel is one of an expensive chain, much in demand for conferences.

The luxurious double bed is UCR. The main door is UL of the bed, with a walk-in closet/dressing room UR. The bathroom leads off UL and a connecting door leads to an adjoining room DR. This door, which opens onstage, can be locked with a key or bolted from either side. There is a small armchair below the closet door and another, with a table beside it, below the bathroom door, DL. There are lamps on two bedside tables, with a phone on the table L of the bed.

Enter NICK. *He is a 51-year-old London Q C, confident and urbane. He is dressed in his suit, and carries a dinner jacket on a hanger. He is ushered in by* CHRISTIAN, *19, the chamber-lad, who carries* NICK'S *suitcase.* CHRISTIAN *is a psychology student, bright and good-looking, working during his vacation.*

CHRISTIAN	Yes indeed, sir. Finest hotel in Birmingham. And this has got to be one of our best rooms.
NICK	Oh yes?
CHRISTIAN	In my opinion. It is the honeymoon suite, after all.
NICK	Is it? They didn't tell me that.
CHRISTIAN	You don't mind, do you sir?
NICK	No, no . . .
CHRISTIAN	Normally kept for honeymooners, of course – being the honeymoon suite – but what with the big conference this weekend we're chock-a-block.
NICK	Yes, of course.
CHRISTIAN	I'm sure you'll find it very comfortable, sir. Just for the one night, I take it?

NICK What?

CHRISTIAN You are with the conference? The lawyers?

NICK Oh. Yes. The conference. Just the one night.

CHRISTIAN (*taking* NICK's *DJ and hanging it up in the closet*) This is the closet, sir. Walk-in. Nice and spacious. (*Crossing to the bathroom.*) Bathroom. Bath, shower, bidet –

NICK What's that door?

CHRISTIAN Room next door, sir. Sometimes these two are let as a pair.

NICK (*trying the door*) But it will be kept locked?

CHRISTIAN Oh yes, sir. No chance of any unwelcome guests after lights out.

NICK Or any welcome ones, presumably.

CHRISTIAN (*enjoying the joke*) No, sir! I'll leave you to it, then.

NICK (*offering a good tip*) Thank you.

CHRISTIAN Thank you, sir. If there's anything else you need, I'm on the twelve-hour shift till midnight. Just dial 9 and ask for Christian.

(*Exit* CHRISTIAN. NICK *takes out his mobile and dials. During the following conversation he puts away his case in the closet and generally checks the facilities.*)

NICK Hello? Mother? It's Nicholas . . . (*Louder*) Nicholas! . . . Yes . . . Yes, I know Hilary's there. That's why I'm ringing . . . No, dear, I don't want to speak to her. I just wanted to make sure she'd arrived safely . . . We arranged it. Hilary said she'd come and see you instead . . . I've got an important conference, Mother . . . In Birmingham . . . Yes, I know it's not far, but . . . Well, we all have to make an effort with our in-laws, Mother . . . It's only for the one night . . . No, I don't need to speak to her... (*Sotto voce.*) Dear God... (*Normal voice.*) Nothing, Mother. Just give Hilary my love and I'll see you next month... Yes... Yes... Goodbye.

(*He sits on the bed to test the spring of the mattress, which is to his satisfaction. Knock. He answers the door. Enter* TONI. *She is a 20-year-old solicitors' secretary, vivacious, bright and very pretty. She carries an overnight bag.*)

NICK   Toni!

TONI   (*coming straight in*) Hi! Ooh, this is very swish.

NICK   You're nice and early.

TONI   I'm always early. Been looking forward to this all week.

NICK   Good journey?

TONI   Yeah, not bad. Train was a bit crowded, though. I don't like that. I get this claustrophobia, you see. (*Putting her arms round his neck.*) So, how are you?

NICK   Fine. I'm fine. (*He gives her a quick kiss on the lips.*)

TONI   (*moving away*) You got away okay, then?

NICK   Yes. It was quite easy, really. Hilary's gone to see my mother. Overnight.

TONI   You sounded very out of breath when you rang.

NICK   Well, I was on my mobile. Out on my run.

TONI   I like a man who keeps fit.

NICK   I couldn't ring from Chambers, and I certainly didn't want to ring from home.

TONI   Puffing away like that. I wondered what you were up to.

NICK   You are very naughty!

TONI	This hotel's great. (*Showing a brochure.*) Have you seen? They've got a gym and everything. Heated swimming pool, jacuzzi and a sauna. And look at the restaurant.
NICK	Ah. Now . . .
TONI	So, what's the plan?
NICK	I thought we could stay up here most of the time, actually. Just you and me. You know.
TONI	Mmm. That sounds nice. (*She starts to unpack, bringing out first a skimpy red dress.*) Do you like this?
NICK	Very much.
TONI	That's for dinner.
NICK	Er . . .
TONI	And this – (*Bringing out her nightie.*) – is for afters.
NICK	Blimey! (TONI *puts her arms round his neck again and kisses him.*) Look, I think there's something I'd better explain. You know I said I had to come to the hotel for a meeting . . .
TONI	Yeah. That's what you told your wife.
NICK	Yes. The thing is, it's true.
TONI	Oh.
NICK	And it's more of a conference than a meeting, really.
TONI	What sort of conference?
NICK	Well, our Head of Chambers wants to be a High Court Judge, you see. Set his heart on it. Can't think why – the money's terrible. Anyway, to cut a long story short, he missed out last year and thinks he's been passed over. So he's decided to try and impress the Lord Chancellor by organising this conference called "Clean

up the Bar". That's one of the new Lord Chancellor's pet subjects.

TONI So this place is going to be crawling with lawyers?

NICK Afraid so.

TONI And you don't want to be seen with me in public, is that it?

NICK No, no . . .

TONI Charming!

NICK It's not that at all.

TONI What's this conference consist of, then?

NICK Well, the main session's this afternoon. I have to be at that –

TONI Oh great.

NICK Then there's a formal dinner this evening, with the Lord Chancellor's big speech.

TONI That'll be nice.

NICK With the final session tomorrow morning.

TONI You haven't organised this very well, have you?

NICK How do you mean?

TONI Well, what about me?

NICK We've got masses of time together. A couple of hours now, plenty of time before dinner and then – the whole night to ourselves.

TONI (*uncertain*) Mm.

NICK You've got the gym, the pool and the sauna while I'm working. And for dinner you can go *à la carte*. Order

	anything you like. The room service here is fabulous. In fact . . . (*He goes to the bedside phone and dials.*)
TONI	What are you doing?
NICK	"Just dial 9 and ask for Christian" . . . Hello? Christian? . . . Champagne for Room 101, please.
TONI	Ooh, bubbly!
NICK	And two glasses. Quick as you can.
TONI	You haven't done this before, have you?
NICK	What do you mean?
TONI	I can tell.
NICK	Is it that obvious? (TONI *gives him a look.*) You know, I could skip this afternoon's session.
TONI	Sounds good to me. (*Just as they go to embrace again,* NICK'S *mobile rings.*)
NICK	Blast! Sorry.
TONI	Leave it.
NICK	Better not . . . (*He answers his phone.*) Hello . . . Hilary! . . . No, darling, I don't want to talk to you . . . I mean, I do want to talk to you, but . . . Well, she got it wrong. I just rang to make sure you'd arrived safely, that's all . . . (TONI *starts getting flirty.*) She can't help it, darling . . . I know . . . Well, please do try . . . (TONI *is getting quite naughty and* NICK *reacts.*) Ah! . . . No, I'm fine. Touch of cramp . . . Look, darling, I must go. Very busy afternoon ahead . . . (*Knock.*) Someone at the door. See you tomorrow. 'Bye, darling . . . 'Bye. (*He makes a decision to turn off his mobile and opens the door.*)
NICK	Ah, Christian. Come in.

(*Enter* CHRISTIAN *with champagne in ice-bucket and glasses on a tray.*)

CHRISTIAN	Sir.
TONI	Hi!
CHRISTIAN	Good afternoon, miss.
NICK	Just set it down over there, would you?
CHRISTIAN	Certainly, sir. (*He unloads the tray.*)
NICK	Don't worry. I'll open it.
CHRISTIAN	Yes, sir. (NICK *tips him.*) Thank you, sir.
TONI	Ooh, Christian.
CHRISTIAN	Yes, miss?
TONI	Got any smoked salmon sandwiches?
CHRISTIAN	Certainly, miss.
	(*Exit* CHRISTIAN.)
TONI	He's nice.
NICK	(*pouring the champagne*) Champagne, "madame"?
TONI	I think I'm beginning to enjoy this.
NICK	Look, I'm ever so sorry about all these arrangements.
TONI	Don't worry. I've got a feeling everything's going to be just fine.
NICK	I hope so.
TONI	So do I.
NICK	(*handing her a glass*) To us!
TONI	(*toasting him*) To us! (*Knock.*) Blimey, he was quick with those sandwiches. Where's the bathroom?
NICK	Through there.

TONI	Don't go away...

(*Exit* TONI *to the bathroom. Another knock.* NICK *opens the door: nobody there. Puzzled, he closes the door. Third knock, which* NICK *realises is from the adjoining room.*)

NICK	Hello?
HUGO	(*off*) Hello.
NICK	Who's that?
HUGO	(*off*) It's me.
NICK	Who's me?
HUGO	(*off*) Hugo.
NICK	Hugo?
HUGO	(*off*) Yes.
NICK	What are you doing in there?
HUGO	(*off*) Let me in.
NICK	I can't.
HUGO	(*off*) Open up, old man.
NICK	I told you, I can't.
HUGO	(*off*) Why not?
NICK	The door's locked.
HUGO	(*off*) Right, I'll come round.
NICK	Dear God.

(*Enter* TONI.)

NICK	Ah...

TONI	Forgot my glass.
NICK	Oh.

(Exit TONI *to the bathroom with her glass. Knock.* NICK *answers the door. Enter* HUGO, *dressed in his suit. He is also 51, a Q C, and he is head of* NICK's *Chambers. They are old friends. In character, however,* HUGO *is* NICK's *opposite: hardworking, but vague and a little naïve.)*

HUGO	Have to do something about getting that door unlocked, old man.
NICK	Ah. No. Can't be done.
HUGO	I'll have a word at the desk.
NICK	Are you next door, then?
HUGO	Yes, quite a stroke of luck. They said they could give us connecting rooms. We can use them as a suite to entertain Sir Harry and do a bit of preparation for the conference. I'll be looking to you for a lot of support this weekend.
NICK	*(appalled)* Will you?
HUGO	*(having a look round)* I say, this room's rather good. Lovely double bed. Couple of mingey twins in mine. This the bathroom?
NICK	Er...
HUGO	*(trying the door)* Door's stuck, d'you know that? *(Knock.)* Someone at the door, old man.
NICK	That'll be the sandwiches.

*(*NICK *opens the door. Enter* CHRISTIAN *with a plate of sandwiches.)*

NICK	Christian.

CHRISTIAN	Your sandwiches, sir.
NICK	Thank you, Christian.
HUGO	(*taking the plate from* CHRISTIAN) Ah. Smoked salmon. Excellent. (*He starts eating.*)
CHRISTIAN	Shall I bring a third glass, sir?
NICK	No.
HUGO	Why? Thinking of joining us, are you?
CHRISTIAN	Er . . . no, sir. Will that be all?
NICK	Yes.
HUGO	No. Bathroom door's stuck. Take a look at it, will you?
CHRISTIAN	(*crossing to the bathroom*) Certainly, sir.
HUGO	Mmm. Lovely. Nick, have a sandwich.
NICK	No. I ordered those for . . . later.
CHRISTIAN	I don't think it's stuck, sir. It's locked.
HUGO	Locked? Of course it's not locked.
NICK	(*looking* CHRISTIAN *square in the eye*) It can't be locked.
CHRISTIAN	Ah.
HUGO	It can't be locked.
CHRISTIAN	No, sir.
HUGO	Silly boy.
NICK	Silly boy.
CHRISTIAN	Silly boy! (*A phone rings in* HUGO's *room, off R.*)
NICK	Is that your phone, Hugo?
HUGO	What?

NICK	Phone. In your room.
HUGO	Ah, phone. In my room. Must be for me. (*Taking the last of the sandwiches and handing the plate to* NICK.) Splendid sandwiches. Thank you very much.

(*Exit* HUGO.)

NICK	A third glass might come in handy, Christian.
CHRISTIAN	Understood, sir.

(*Enter* TONI *from the bathroom.*)

TONI	Ooh, no window in there and I get ever so claustrophobic. I go all sweaty and think I'm having a heart attack. It's always worse when I'm in a strange place. I suddenly feel it coming on and I just have to get out. (*She takes three deep breaths.*) Better now.
CHRISTIAN	Fascinating.
NICK	Yes, fascinating. Now, Toni –
CHRISTIAN	Claustrophobia. Causes: paediatric panic, adolescent anxiety, or chronic crypto-cranial enclosure trauma in the adult. Effects: fear of cupboards, bathrooms and aircraft. Therapy: voluntary and incremental immersion in the phobic environment.
TONI	Ooh...
NICK	Yes, well...
CHRISTIAN	The trick is, give yourself a minute longer each time.
TONI	I could only do three minutes in there. Three mins max.
CHRISTIAN	So – try four next time.
TONI	Okay.
CHRISTIAN	You'll be amazed.

ACT ONE

TONI How do you know all this?

CHRISTIAN Psychology. Third year.

TONI Ooh...

NICK Look –

TONI Hey, were those my sandwiches?

NICK Sorry. Hugo ate them.

TONI Hugo?

NICK Christian. More smoked salmon sandwiches, there's a good chap.

TONI Who's Hugo?

CHRISTIAN Certainly, sir. And a third glass.

(*Exit* CHRISTIAN.)

TONI Who's Hugo?

NICK He's the fellow I told you about. He's running the conference.

TONI What was he doing in our room?

NICK I don't know really.

TONI And why did he eat my sandwiches?

NICK Look, he'll be back in a minute.

TONI What?

NICK He just nipped next door to take a phone call.

TONI Well, I don't want to see him.

NICK And I don't want him to see you.

TONI Why not?

NICK	Because he'd disapprove, that's why. (*Knock.*)
TONI	Is that him?
NICK	Probably. (*Topping up her glass.*) You just nip back in the bathroom and I'll get rid of him.
TONI	Promise?
NICK	Promise.
TONI	All right, but don't be long. Remember, four mins max.

(*Knock. Exit* TONI *to the bathroom.*)

HUGO	(*off*) Nick!

(NICK *opens the door.*)

NICK	Ah. Hugo.

(*Enter* HUGO. *He still doesn't notice* TONI'S *clothes on the bed.*)

HUGO	That was Sir Harry. I think he's half-cut.
NICK	Is he here?
HUGO	No, he's holed up in some canalside pub off the M42 doing his "Lord-Chancellor-meets-the-ordinary-drinking-man" bit.
NICK	Oh God.
HUGO	Claims he's surrounded by a dozen awe-struck yeomen of middle England, tucking into rare roast beef and Yorkshire pudding, hanging on his every syllable.
NICK	Yeah. One deaf fisherman and a mangey collie trapped in the snug and bored rigid, reactionary old fart.
HUGO	That's no way to speak of your father-in-law.
NICK	It's the only way to speak of my father-in-law.

HUGO   It's all very well for you. You don't want to be a judge. You do know why I've organised this conference, don't you?

NICK   Yes, but Hugo –

HUGO   To convince Sir Harry that I'm sound judge material, that's why.

NICK   Toadying, I call it.

HUGO   Call it what you like. Why do you think I've invited him to give the opening address this afternoon? Why do you think I've asked him to make the after-dinner speech tonight?

NICK   Hugo –

HUGO   And more to the point, why do you think I've called the conference "Clean up the Bar"? You know the Lord Chancellor still holds all the power.

NICK   Hugo. May I say something?

HUGO   Of course.

NICK   You won't be offended?

HUGO   No. (*He starts toying absent-mindedly with an item of* TONI'S *underwear.*)

NICK   I think this conference is a great idea, really I do. The old man's going to be highly impressed. And flattered, come to that. But it won't make a scrap of difference to your prospects of promotion. You know Sir Harry's views as well as I do. You're a single man 'of a certain age', Hugo, and we all know what that's supposed to mean.

HUGO   Do we?

NICK   Oh come on . . .

HUGO	What?
NICK	(*spelling it out in a matter-of-fact manner*) G – A – Y.
HUGO	Gay? Oh, for goodness sake, Nick, don't be so bloody ridiculous. The prejudice of some people nowadays.
NICK	It's not my prejudice, Hugo –
HUGO	It really makes my blood boil!
NICK	(*gently taking underwear from* HUGO) Look, I know it's nonsense, but Hilary's mentioned it once or twice. About how you . . . well . . . might be.
HUGO	Nick, you're not listening to me.
NICK	It wouldn't make any difference to us, you know.
HUGO	No, nor to me neither. I abhor that kind of prejudice. It just so happens that I'm not, that's all.
NICK	Fine, fine.
HUGO	(*more relaxed*) I nearly got married once, as a matter of fact.
NICK	I never knew that.
HUGO	Well, it didn't work out. And I'm far too set in my ways now. Quite happy with my concerts, my bell-ringing and my fish. I'm fully prepared to arrange conferences to enhance my professional reputation, but I'm damned if I'm going to start getting married simply to satisfy one bigoted Lord Chancellor, Sir Harry or no Sir Harry.
NICK	I'm not suggesting for one moment that you should.
HUGO	Mind you, I look at Hilary sometimes and I think, "you lucky devil". She's beautiful, intelligent, a fabulous cook – that dinner before Christmas! – and your two lovely boys. And you've been so sensible, Nick. God knows, there must have been temptations. I do admire you for that.

ACT ONE

>(*Knock.* NICK *answers the door. Enter* CHRISTIAN *with a second plate of sandwiches and a third glass.*)

NICK Christian.

CHRISTIAN Your sandwiches, sir.

NICK Thank you.

HUGO What, more smoked salmon?

CHRISTIAN Yes, sir.

HUGO Splendid. Bring them over here.

NICK Hugo . . .

CHRISTIAN Yes, sir.

HUGO Thank you very much.

>(CHRISTIAN *hands the plate to* HUGO *and goes to pour a glass of champagne. He has taken an instant liking to* HUGO.)

CHRISTIAN Champagne, sir?

HUGO No, no. Too early in the day for me.

CHRISTIAN Sure I can't tempt you, sir?

HUGO Quite sure, thanks.

CHRISTIAN Oh go on.

HUGO I beg your pardon?

CHRISTIAN Spoil yourself!

HUGO Oh . . . all right. Just a small one. (CHRISTIAN *pours.* HUGO *and* NICK *exchange glances.*) Thank you.

CHRISTIAN My pleasure, sir.

>(*Exit* CHRISTIAN.)

HUGO	Funny boy.
NICK	I think he was giving you the glad eye, Hugo.
HUGO	(*amazed*) Do you?
NICK	Well, you know what they say: "Hotel and Catering".
HUGO	What?
NICK	You know. (*With appropriate but inoffensive gesture: perhaps one hand on his hip, the other miming carrying a tray above his head.*) "Hotel and Catering".
HUGO	Good Lord.
NICK	Yes.
HUGO	But I'm old enough to be his father.
	(*Enter* TONI *from the bathroom, gasping.*)
TONI	Ooh, I think I did it. Four minutes.
HUGO	Who's this?
TONI	Hi, I'm Toni. Pleased to meet you.
HUGO	Nick?
NICK	Er...
TONI	And I know who you are. You're Hugo.
HUGO	Good God.
TONI	And you're very naughty.
HUGO	What?
TONI	You've been eating my sandwiches, haven't you?
HUGO	I don't believe this.
NICK	Look, Hugo...

HUGO	Don't you "Look Hugo" me. (*Taking* NICK *aside.*) Are you mad? Bringing a girl here, this weekend, to this hotel? What if Hilary were to find out?
NICK	She won't. She's at my mother's. She won't turn up here.
HUGO	And what about my reputation? And the reputation of Chambers? Have you considered that? The title of this conference is "Clean up the Bar", in case you'd forgotten. You could ruin everything. (*Knock.*) Who is it?
GERALD	(*off*) It's Gerald.
NICK	Oh my God.
TONI	Who's Gerald?
HUGO	(*to* NICK) You'd better get her back in the bathroom.
TONI	Why?
NICK	It's Gerald.
TONI	Who's Gerald?
HUGO	Sir Harry's PA, minder – (*Knock.*)
NICK	Spy.
HUGO	It's his job to tell Sir Harry everything.
NICK	And from what I've heard, he does.
TONI	Who's Sir Harry?
HUGO	The Lord Chancellor, that's who.
TONI	Ooh, a bigwig!
HUGO	The biggest.

NICK	Bigot, right-wing populist and self-appointed guardian of public morals.
TONI	Ooh.
NICK	And more to the point, my father-in-law.
TONI	Blimey. (*Knock.*)
GERALD	(*off*) Hello.
HUGO	Just one moment, Gerald.
NICK	Into the bathroom. Quick.
TONI	All right, but don't be long. I can only do . . . five minutes. Five mins max.

(NICK *bundles* TONI *into the bathroom. He then opens the door. Enter* GERALD. *He is 25, a fast-track civil servant in the Lord Chancellor's Department. He is thorough, organised and very dull.*)

NICK	Gerald.
GERALD	Good afternoon, Mr Barnes. I did try your room next door but receiving no reply I took the liberty of trying Mr Willmott's. I'm afraid I am the bearer of heavy tidings. Sir Henry Lumsden-Clark appears to have been unavoidably delayed.
HUGO	Who? Oh, Sir Harry. Yes, we know. Something about a pub off the M42.
GERALD	He did telephone me from a public house, sir. Stopped off, I understand, for a beef sandwich and a mineral water.
NICK	Ha!
HUGO	What can we do for you, Gerald?
GERALD	Well, sir, it occurred to me that in the unfortunate – and unlikely – event of the Lord Chancellor failing to arrive in time to deliver this afternoon's opening address, you

	might like to familiarise yourself with the text of his speech, a fair copy of which I happen to have on my person, sir, in case you find it incumbent upon yourself to take the Lord Chancellor's place. (*He hands* HUGO *a copy of the speech.*)
HUGO	I can't introduce the conference. I'm chairing the forum afterwards.
NICK	Might have to do both, old chap.
GERALD	I think Mr Willmott does have a point there, sir, if I may be so bold. It might be advisable to make a quick perusal of the final text. In the course of the next seventeen minutes or so.
HUGO	(*looking at his watch*) Good Lord.
GERALD	(*noticing* TONI'S *bag and clothing*) Will Mrs Willmott be attending the forum, sir?
NICK	Who?
GERALD	Your wife, sir.
NICK	Ah . . .
GERALD	I hadn't realised she'd be with us.
HUGO	(*in another world*) She's not.
NICK	(*appalled*) Hugo . . .
GERALD	No?
HUGO	She's staying with Mr Willmott's mother.
NICK	Hugo!
HUGO	And she won't turn up here.
GERALD	Sorry, I assumed –
NICK	What did you assume?

GERALD	Well, that...
NICK	That I had a lady friend, Gerald?
GERALD	No, sir. But –
NICK	Come on, Hugo.
HUGO	What?
NICK	You'll have to come clean.
HUGO	Eh?
NICK	We're all men of the world here, aren't we, Gerald?
GERALD	I don't really think it's any of my business, sir.
NICK	Hugo?
HUGO	What do you want me to say?
NICK	What Mr Barnes is trying to tell you, Gerald, is that not only has he organised the conference this weekend, but he's taken the opportunity to line himself up with a bit of totty.
HUGO	Totty?
NICK	Isn't that so, Hugo?
HUGO	You...!
GERALD	(*to* HUGO) So this is your room is it, sir?
HUGO	Er...
NICK	Yes.
HUGO	Nick!
NICK	It was my room, but when I arrived and got wind of what Mr Barnes was up to, I thought "What are chums for?" and I offered it to him.
HUGO	Did you really?

NICK   This room being a double and next door a mere twin.

GERALD   I see.

NICK   I shouldn't be surprised, you know, Gerald, if this didn't improve Mr Barnes's promotion prospects, given Sir Harry's well-publicised views on single gentlemen of a certain age.

HUGO   I don't believe this.

GERALD   No, sir. Mr Willmott could well be right. The new Lord Chancellor is very down on that sort of thing.

(*Enter* TONI *from the bathroom.*)

TONI   (*to* NICK) I'm ever so sorry. I couldn't last any longer. I told you, five mins max.

NICK   Here she is. (*Beat.*)

TONI   Do I get introduced or what?

NICK   Hugo?

HUGO   Me? Oh, yes. Gerald, this is Miss . . . er . . .

NICK   (*sotto voce to* HUGO) Taylor.

HUGO   Taylor.

GERALD   (*shaking her hand*) Gerald Blunt. Pleased to meet you, Miss Taylor.

TONI   (*nervously*) Hi.

GERALD   Mr Willmott's told me all about you.

TONI   Has he?

GERALD   And I would venture to suggest that Sir Harry will find this development very much to his liking.

TONI   Who, the bigot?

GERALD	I beg your pardon?
TONI	I mean, bigwig. (*The phone rings off R in* HUGO's *room.*)
HUGO	That'll be my phone.
NICK	No, Hugo – my phone.
HUGO	No, mine.
NICK	Next door, Hugo. My phone.
HUGO	Oh I see. Your phone. Next door. Yes. Well, better go and answer it, hadn't you?
NICK	Yes, Hugo. (*He makes to go.*)
HUGO	Nick.
NICK	What?
HUGO	(*laid-back*) You'll need your key.
NICK	(*taking key or pass*) Thank you, Hugo.
	(*Exit* NICK.)
GERALD	Just before I go, sir, and leave you two on your own together –
TONI	Eh?
GERALD	The Lord Chancellor – (*To* TONI.) that's the bigwig to you, miss – has asked me to arrange a private meeting between the two of you –
TONI	What? With me?
GERALD	(*patiently*) Er, no, miss. Between Mr Barnes and the Lord Chancellor. A private meeting between the two of them to finalise the contents of his after-dinner speech, sir, this meeting to be held at seven o'clock sharp here, in this room.

TONI	Here? This is my room.
GERALD	Yes, I know, miss. And it had occurred to me, with the distraction you might pose both to your 'partner' and indeed to Sir Harry himself –
TONI	What's he on about?
GERALD	– that you might want to avail yourself of Mr Willmott's facilities –
TONI	Ooh, you cheeky thing!
GERALD	– for the duration of the aforementioned meeting.
HUGO	He means you could go next door.
TONI	But he said Mr Willmott. That's Nick. He's not next door.
GERALD	Yes, he is. He went to answer the phone.
HUGO	And he's being a very long time about it.
GERALD	(*crossing to the connecting door*) I would venture to suggest that it might be useful if we could find a way of unlocking this door.
TONI	No!
HUGO	Good idea.
	(*Enter* NICK.)
NICK	That was Sir Harry. He wants a quick word, Hugo.
HUGO	Quick? That'll be the day. (*He makes to go.*)
NICK	Hugo.
HUGO	What?
NICK	(*laid-back*) You'll need my key.
HUGO	(*taking key or pass*) Thank you, Nick.

(*Exit* HUGO.)

GERALD What word from the Lord Chancellor, sir?

NICK Hard to tell, really. I reckon he's well into his third bottle of mineral water.

GERALD Dear, oh dear. Just as well I brought his speech up for Mr Barnes. I'd better get on, sir. I shall see you later, downstairs.

NICK Thank you, Gerald.

GERALD Miss Taylor.

(*Exit* GERALD.)

TONI Do you know something, Nicholas?

NICK What's that, my darling?

TONI (*exploding*) I am really pissed off! It's like Piccadilly Circus round here. First Hugo, then this Gerald, and now I'm being packed off next door while you all have your meetings.

NICK What are you talking about?

TONI I'm sorry, Nicholas, but I've had enough. I'm off. (*She starts packing her bag.*)

NICK No, wait. Toni, please. I'm sorry. There won't be any more interruptions. Trust me.

TONI You said that before.

NICK I mean it.

TONI I wanted this to be just you and me.

NICK And so it shall be, my darling.

TONI No more Hugos?

NICK	No more Hugos.
TONI	No more Geralds?
NICK	No more Geralds.
TONI	And no Sir Harrys?
NICK	Definitely no Sir Harrys. From now on, just us.
TONI	Promise?
NICK	Promise. (*They kiss lightly.*)
TONI	I am still worried about your wife.
NICK	My wife's at my mother's. I told you. (*Knock. Stopping dead.*) Who is it?
CHRISTIAN	(*off*) Christian.
NICK	It's only Christian. (*He opens the door.*) Come in, Christian.
CHRISTIAN	Just come to sort out that door, sir.
	(CHRISTIAN *goes straight to the connecting door and unlocks it. During the following he opens it to check it and closes it again.*)
NICK	What are you doing?
CHRISTIAN	Orders from downstairs, sir.
HUGO	(*off: heard as the door is opened*) And the same to you, Sir Harry.
TONI	I can't bear this.
CHRISTIAN	Miss?
TONI	It's getting worse.
CHRISTIAN	Try taking deep breaths.
	(*Exit* CHRISTIAN. *Enter* HUGO *from the adjoining room.*)

HUGO	I knew it. Says he's going to be late. He can't find his car now. The whole thing's a complete disaster.
NICK	Hugo, calm down.
HUGO	We're due to start in ten minutes. What are we going to do?
NICK	Simple, old chap. You'll have to give the opening address yourself.
HUGO	Blasted nuisance.
NICK	(*handing him the speech*) Thanks be to Gerald.
HUGO	But I can't chair the forum as well.
NICK	Ask someone else.
HUGO	Who?
NICK	No idea.
HUGO	Would you do it?
NICK	Ah, well ...
HUGO	You'd be perfect.
NICK	I had other plans this afternoon.
HUGO	I am pretty stuck, old man.
NICK	Well ...
HUGO	Please.
NICK	Oh all right.
TONI	Nicholas!
HUGO	Terrific.
TONI	Terrific.

NICK	(*to* TONI) I'm sorry.
HUGO	Nick. We don't really have to change rooms, do we?
TONI	Eh?
NICK	No, no. That's just what we had to tell Gerald.
TONI	(*to* NICK) What's he on about?
HUGO	I suppose I had better just have a look at what the old bugger was planning to say. (*He immerses himself in the speech.*)
TONI	Nicholas, you promised. (*The bedside phone rings.* NICK *answers it.*)
NICK	Hello? . . . Yes, it is . . . My wife? Yes, of course I'll speak to her . . . Darling! Everything all right? . . . Oh dear, did she? . . . She didn't? . . . She did . . . How very annoying . . . Where? . . . What do you mean, "Reception"? . . . Darling? . . . Hello? Darling are you there? (*He puts the phone down. To* TONI:) That was Hilary. She's here. She's coming up!
HUGO	Everything all right, old man?
NICK	It's Hilary. She's on her way up.
HUGO	Is she here?
NICK	Yes.
HUGO	(*preoccupied*) Jolly good. Look, I must be off. Give her my love, will you?
NICK	No, no, Hugo. Don't go. What am I going to do?
HUGO	I know what I'd do.
NICK	What?
HUGO	Get rid of the girl.
NICK	Brilliant.

TONI	Charming.
NICK	Toni, into the bathroom. Quick.
TONI	I can't. Not again. Not yet.
NICK	Oh God.
TONI	I suppose I could go next door.
NICK	Good girl. All right with you, Hugo?
HUGO	(*vaguely*) What?
NICK	If Toni uses your room for a moment?
HUGO	What for?
	(*Knock.*)
NICK	(*in frustration*) Hugo!
HILARY	(*off*) Darling!
TONI	Ooh...
	(*Exit* TONI *to the adjoining room.*)
NICK	Champagne, Hugo.
HUGO	Not just now, thank you.
NICK	Get rid of it.
HILARY	(*off*) It's me.
HUGO	Oh. Right.
	(HUGO *hides the bottle and glasses behind the table.*)
NICK	Get a move on!
HUGO	Ready!

NICK	(*opening the door*) Darling! (TONI *opens the connecting door.* NICK *shuts the main door in* HILARY'S *face.*)
TONI	My bag!
NICK	(*to* HUGO) Her bag!
HUGO	What?
NICK	Bag!
HUGO	Ah! (*He picks up the bag and throws it to* TONI.) Bag!
TONI	Ooh!
	(*Exit* TONI. NICK *opens the door.*)
NICK	(*over-expansive*) Darling!
	(*Enter* HILARY. *She is 42, attractive and down-to-earth. She carries a small overnight case.*)
HILARY	Hello, darling.
NICK	Darling!
HILARY	Are you all right?
NICK	Fantastic to see you!
HILARY	I thought you'd be pleased.
HUGO	(*putting his hand up*) Excuse me.
HILARY	Hi, Hugo.
HUGO	Hello, Hilary. Er, Nick –
NICK	And how are you, darling?
HILARY	About the same as I was at breakfast.
NICK	Marvellous. That's good news. Isn't it, Hugo?
HUGO	Yes. I really think I should go down.
NICK	No, no. Don't go, Hugo. Hilary's only just arrived.

HUGO   Oh dear.

NICK   Haven't you, darling?

HILARY   You know I have. Darling, I really think –

NICK   So . . . How's mother?

HILARY   Oh God! I hadn't been in the house five minutes before she started asking me when I was leaving. "Where's Nicholas?" she kept saying. "When's he coming?" She didn't offer me lunch and there wasn't a sniff of a drink. Just started clipping her toenails before making herself a revolting cup of soup and going off to listen to Gardeners Question Time. With her headphones on. I tell you, I felt about as welcome as a fish in a fruit salad.

NICK   So, you thought you'd escape for the afternoon, did you?

HILARY   I'm not spending another second in the company of that malignant old bat. No, I've decided to treat myself to the shops and then I've arranged to have supper with Fiona. You remember, Fiona Plum, my friend from college. The one you never liked. Then, who knows? It's ages since we spent a night away together, just the two of us. And they told me downstairs that this was the honeymoon suite!

NICK   Lovely, darling. So . . . what sort of time do you reckon you'll be back? Roughly . . .

HILARY   Ooh, elevenish. No earlier.

NICK   No earlier.

HUGO   Hil old thing, look, I don't mean to be rude, but we've got an important session starting at two.

HILARY   Sure. Sorry. Just need to whizz to the loo. Through there, is it? (*She makes to go through the connecting door.*)

HUGO/NICK No!

NICK	This way, darling.
HILARY	Shan't be a tick.
	(*Exit* HILARY *to the bathroom.*)
HUGO	When I said "Get rid of the girl", old man...
NICK	(*taking* HILARY'S *case and putting it in the closet*) Yes, yes, I know what you're going to say.
HUGO	Well?
NICK	She can't stay now. Do you think I'm stupid or something?
HUGO	You tell me.
NICK	I do wish you'd stop interfering.
HUGO	Ha!
	(*Enter* TONI *from the adjoining room.*)
TONI	Has she gone?
NICK	No.
HUGO	Not yet.
TONI	Ooh...
	(*Exit* TONI *to the adjoining room. Enter* HILARY *from the bathroom.*)
HILARY	Well, I'm off. Have a super conference and don't do anything I wouldn't do. (*Kissing* NICK.) See you later, honeymooner.
NICK	Elevenish.
HILARY	Certainly no earlier. 'Bye, boys.
HUGO	'Bye.

NICK	'Bye.

(*Exit* HILARY.)

NICK	Gosh, is that the time? You're going to be late, Hugo.

(HUGO *crosses to the connecting door.*)

NICK	What are you doing?
HUGO	(*opening the door*) Miss Taylor.
TONI	(*off*) Is it safe?
HUGO	Would you come in here for a moment, please?

(*Enter* TONI.)

TONI	Has she gone?
NICK	Yes.
TONI	Ooh, that was close.
HUGO	Mr Willmott's got something he'd like to say to you.
NICK	Have I?
HUGO	You know damned well you have.
NICK	Ah. Yes. Now look, Toni. We've been having a little chat and we think this is all getting a bit . . . silly.
TONI	"We"?
NICK	Well, I. I think, given all that's happened, that perhaps you'd better just . . . er . . . leave.
TONI	Piss off, you mean.
NICK	Well . . .
TONI	Charming.
NICK	Toni, I'm really sorry.

TONI	I'll go and get my things. (*She goes off angrily to the adjoining room.*)
HUGO	All for the best, old man. Now, I've got to dash.
NICK	See you down there, Hugo.
HUGO	Right.
	(*Exit* HUGO. *Enter* TONI.)
TONI	Nicholas Willmott, you are one complete shit! Never –
NICK	Joke.
TONI	– in my whole life –
NICK	Joke.
TONI	What?
NICK	It was a joke.
TONI	You mean . . . ?
NICK	Yes!
TONI	Ooh, you terror. You are a terror. I really thought . . .
NICK	I know.
TONI	You little bugger!
NICK	Come here. (*They embrace.*) Now remember, it's all yours: sauna, gym, jacuzzi . . .
TONI	Indoor pool . . .
NICK	Room service.
TONI	"Just dial 9 and ask for Christian".
NICK	And I'll be back at five.
TONI	We've got plenty of time before dinner, haven't we?
NICK	Loads.

TONI	And what time do you reckon your dinner will finish?
NICK	Oh . . . tennish.
TONI	No earlier?
NICK	No . . . tennish . . .

Scene Two

Saturday 6.00 PM.

NICK *is dozing on the bed, dressed in his suit trousers and open-necked shirt.* TONI'S *dress and underwear are on the bed. Knock on the connecting door.*

HUGO	(*off*) Nick? Nick?
NICK	(*stirring*) What? (*Knock.*)
HUGO	(*off*) Nick!
NICK	Hugo?
HUGO	(*off*) They've locked this blasted door again.
NICK	(*getting up to unbolt the door*) Oh God.
HUGO	Can you let me in?
	(*Enter* HUGO, *dressed in his dinner jacket.*)
HUGO	They gave you the key then, did they?
NICK	No, I bolted it. Thought I'd have a quick nap. (*Pointedly.*) And a bit of privacy.
HUGO	Sorry, old man. Just came to congratulate you on the way you chaired the forum. Superb.
NICK	(*crossing to the bathroom to have a quick wash and a gargle*) Yes, I thought it went rather well.
HUGO	Trust Sir Harry to waltz in five minutes before the end and get a round of applause.

NICK	Who do you think started that off?
HUGO	Don't imagine I didn't notice. If anyone's getting a judgeship out of this, it'll be you.
NICK	(*returning to put on his shoes*) Why does he insist on wearing that god-awful suit? Looks like he's going deer-stalking.
HUGO	At least he made it.
NICK	Silly old sod.
HUGO	And thank God you got rid of that girl. (*Noticing* TONI's *clothes.*) Good Lord.
NICK	Hugo, it's not what you think . . .
HUGO	She's left her clothes behind.
NICK	Er, no, Hugo.
HUGO	What?
NICK	She's still here.
HUGO	You said you were getting rid of her.
NICK	Well . . .
HUGO	Nick, you haven't . . . you know. Have you?
NICK	Chance'd be a fine thing.
HUGO	Where is she now?
NICK	In the gym, Hugo. Limbering up.
HUGO	(*shocked*) Limbering up? (*Knock.*)
NICK	That'll be her now.
HUGO	You seem very relaxed about this.

(NICK *opens the door. Enter* TONI, *fresh from the gym.*)

NICK	Toni. Hi.
TONI	Hi!
NICK	How was the gym?
TONI	Great. And I had this fab jacuzzi. We could have one together later on if you like.
NICK	Sounds fun.
TONI	I'm starving. I saw that Christian downstairs and ordered more of those smoked salmon sandwiches. (*Noticing* HUGO.) Oh. Hello, Hugo. (*Aside, reprovingly.*) Nick!
NICK	Hugo popped in to congratulate me on this afternoon's little effort. He's just off, aren't you, Hugo?
TONI	I'm going to the bathroom to freshen up. (*To* HUGO.) It's getting better, you know.
HUGO	Really?
TONI	Mm. Six minutes now. Six mins max.
	(*Exit* TONI *to the bathroom.*)
HUGO	You are sailing very close to the wind, do you know that?
NICK	I'll mind my business, Hugo, and I'll thank you to mind yours. All right?
HUGO	Someone's got to say it, old man.
NICK	I'll see you at dinner.
HUGO	Haven't you forgotten Sir Harry?
NICK	See him at dinner too, presumably.
HUGO	No. Gerald has arranged a meeting between Sir Harry and me for seven o'clock this evening.

NICK	You've got plenty of time then, Hugo, haven't you? Off you go.
HUGO	In my room.
NICK	Fine. I should get the drinks in if I were you. He's bound to want a snifter or two before dinner. And you know him. Always early when there's booze about.
HUGO	(*spelling it out*) My room, Nick.
NICK	So?
HUGO	It used to be your room, remember? But when you arrived and got wind of what I was up to with my bit of "totty", you thought, "What are friends for?" and offered it to me.
NICK	That's only what we had to tell Gerald –
HUGO	Who tells Sir Harry everything. Remember?
NICK	Ah.
HUGO	Which gives you less than fifteen minutes to get yourself dressed for dinner, clear this room of Toni Totty's bra and panties, and pack her off back to wherever it was she came from. (*Knock.*)
NICK	Who is it?
CHRISTIAN	(*off*) Christian.
NICK	Come in, Christian.
	(*Enter* CHRISTIAN *with a plate of smoked salmon sandwiches.*)
CHRISTIAN	(*to* NICK) Good evening, sir.
HUGO	Ah, the man with the smoked salmon. Splendid.
CHRISTIAN	(*to* HUGO) Hello again, sir. Would you care for a sandwich?

HUGO	(*taking one*) I think you can tempt me. Thank you very much.
NICK	Hugo.
HUGO	Mm? (*Behind* CHRISTIAN'S *back,* NICK *whistles and makes the "Hotel and Catering" gesture.*) Ah.
CHRISTIAN	Your favourite, I believe, sir.
HUGO	Yes, I am quite partial.
CHRISTIAN	I can tell.
HUGO	Can you really?
CHRISTIAN	It's a pleasure being of service to you, sir.
NICK	Thank you, Christian.
CHRISTIAN	Thank you, sir.
	(*Exit* CHRISTIAN. HUGO *finishes all the sandwiches during the following.*)
HUGO	That really is a very nice young man.
NICK	Not turning a touch "Hotel and Catering" ourselves, are we, Hugo?
HUGO	Don't be silly.
NICK	That's all you need, this weekend.
HUGO	So, what are you going to do?
NICK	Do about what?
HUGO	The girl, you fool.
NICK	Well, if Sir Harry's coming up here, I'll have to get rid of her, won't I? My father-in-law. Can you imagine?
HUGO	I'm sure you're doing the right thing, old man.

NICK	You're a good friend, Hugo. (*Opening the connecting door.*) Now, off you go. I'll give you a knock when it's all clear.
HUGO	Good man.

(*Exit* HUGO. NICK *knocks on the bathroom door.*)

NICK	Toni!
TONI	(*off*) Has he gone?
NICK	Yes. Hurry up. (*Beat.*) Hurry up!

(*Enter* TONI, *carrying her gym gear and dressed in bra and panties.*)

TONI	Ooh, you are eager.
NICK	No. I mean – yes, of course I'm eager. But there's been a slight change of plan.
TONI	Not again.
NICK	It appears that Gerald has arranged a meeting here between Hugo and Sir Harry.
TONI	I know.
NICK	Do you?
TONI	Yes, but that's not till seven. We've still got three quarters of an hour. You don't need longer than that, do you? Not the first time?
NICK	Er... I'm not sure, really.
TONI	(*getting amorous*) Well then...
NICK	No, no. The point is, Sir Harry's very unpredictable. He could turn up at any minute. So I thought, while they're having their meeting in here, you and I could slip off together next door and er... well.
TONI	Has he been at my sandwiches again?

NICK	Yes.
TONI	Ooh, the little tinker.
NICK	So – you get dressed.
TONI	Dressed? (NICK *hands* TONI *her dress and starts bundling the rest of her clothes into her bag.*)
NICK	Yes. Listen. (TONI *puts her dress down on the bed, goes to the phone and dials 9.*) What are you doing?
TONI	Nothing. Go on.
NICK	You get dressed . . .
TONI	Hello, could I speak to Christian?
NICK	Toni!
TONI	It's okay, I'm listening.
NICK	You get dressed . . .
TONI	Hi, Christian . . .
NICK	. . . pack as if you're leaving . . .
TONI	It's me in room 101 . . .
NICK	. . . wait in the corridor while I bring Hugo in here ready for Sir Harry . . .
TONI	Can I have some more of those sandwiches, please? . . .
NICK	. . . then I can let you in next door as arranged . . .
TONI	Thanks ever so much, Christian . . .
NICK	. . . and Bob's your uncle!
TONI	'Bye. (*To* NICK.) Why do I have to wait in the corridor? Why can't I go straight through?
NICK	Because Hugo mustn't see you. I told him you'd gone.
TONI	You're very naughty.

NICK	We'll have to be extra quiet.
TONI	(*whispering*) All the more fun! (*Knock.*)
NICK	Who is it?
SIR HARRY	(*off*) Lumsden-Clark here.
NICK	(*whispering*) It's him.
TONI	(*whispering*) Is it him?
NICK	(*whispering*) Yes.
TONI	(*whispering*) Sir Harry?
NICK	(*whispering*) Yes.
TONI	(*loudly*) Ooh!
NICK	Shh!
SIR HARRY	(*off*) Hugo? Are you there?
TONI	Shall I hide in the bathroom?
NICK	Quickly. Yes.
TONI	I can't stay in there very long.
NICK	I know.
TONI	Seven mins max. (*Louder knock.*)
	(*Exit* TONI *to the bathroom.*)
SIR HARRY	(*off*) Let me in!
NICK	Just a moment, Sir Harry.
SIR HARRY	(*off*) Who the devil's that? Nick? (NICK *opens the connecting door.*)
NICK	Hugo!
SIR HARRY	(*off*) Hugo?
HUGO	(*off*) All clear, old man?

NICK	Quickly! It's Sir Harry. He's here.
	(*Enter* HUGO.)
HUGO	My God, he is early.
SIR HARRY	(*off*) Hugo, is that you?
HUGO	Yes.
SIR HARRY	(*off*) Then open this confounded door!
HUGO	Just coming, Sir Harry.
NICK	No, Hugo. Wait.
HUGO	What's the matter?
NICK	She's still here.
HUGO	Who? Totty?
NICK	Yes. No. Toni. Yes.
HUGO	What do you mean, "here"? Where?
NICK	There.
HUGO	In the bathroom?
NICK	Yes.
HUGO	You ass! (*Very loud knocking.*)
SIR HARRY	(*off*) What the blazes is going on in there?
NICK	Look, you let the old man in. And as soon as you can, get him next door.
HUGO	How?
NICK	I don't know. Show him the view or something.
HUGO	View?
SIR HARRY	(*off*) I am not a man who likes to be kept waiting!

NICK	And while he's in there, I'll smuggle Toni out of the bathroom and get her away. (*More knocking.*)
SIR HARRY	(*off*) Will someone open this bloody door!
NICK	Well. Go on, Hugo.
HUGO	What?
NICK	Open the bloody door.
HUGO	Coming, Sir Harry.
	(*Enter* TONI *from the bathroom.*)
TONI	I forgot my dress.
HUGO	I say!
NICK	Hugo. Dress. (*He throws the dress to* HUGO *who throws it to* TONI.)
HUGO	Dress. Yes.
	(*Exit* TONI *to the bathroom.*)
SIR HARRY	(*off*) Hugo!
	(HUGO *opens the door.*)
HUGO	Sir Harry!
	(*Enter* SIR HARRY, *with* GERALD *in tow.* SIR HARRY, *66, is the newly-appointed Lord Chancellor. He is extrovert, domineering and dressed in a loud check suit.*)
SIR HARRY	About bloody time too! Wondered what the hell you were up to. Want to be a bit careful about that sort of thing, you know, two chaps alone together in a hotel bedroom without a chaperone, what? Ha! "Clean up the Bar!" That's what it's all about. No smoke without fire, eh, Gerald?
GERALD	No, Lord Chancellor.
SIR HARRY	Well, Hugo, it all seems to be going rather well. Sorry I was a bit *en retard* earlier on. Dropped into this very

amusing little hostelry by the canal on the way up. Found myself mobbed by Joe Public and his lady wife Josephine. Wanted my opinion on every blasted subject from flogging to capital punishment. Mind you, that didn't take long, eh, Gerald?

GERALD
No, Lord Chancellor.

SIR HARRY
What do you mean, you fool? You weren't even there.

GERALD
No, Lord Chancellor.

SIR HARRY
Then why are you interrupting?

GERALD
Don't know, Lord Chancellor.

SIR HARRY
Got caught out, though. Now here's a story for you. Couple of young chaps in the snug got chatting. Bought me a pint. Seemed perfectly nice. Scottish. Got on famously. One of them even smoked a pipe. Turned out they were a pair of bloody Australians! I couldn't get out of there fast enough.

HUGO
I thought you said they were Scottish.

SIR HARRY
Australian. The other way. (*He makes an upside-down gesture.*) Say no more.

HUGO
Eh?

NICK
"Hotel and Catering", Hugo.

HUGO
Oh. I see. (*Knock.*)

SIR HARRY
Come!

(*Enter* CHRISTIAN.)

CHRISTIAN
You ordered more sandwiches, sir.

SIR HARRY
Splendid. Bring 'em over here.

CHRISTIAN
(*to* HUGO) Anything for you, sir?

SIR HARRY
Yes. Bottle of bubbly. Quick as you like.

CHRISTIAN
Yes, sir.

SIR HARRY	And four glasses.
GERALD	Not for me, Lord Chancellor.
SIR HARRY	What?
GERALD	I don't drink, Lord Chancellor.
SIR HARRY	Nonsense. What are you? Course you drink.
GERALD	Yes, Lord Chancellor.
SIR HARRY	Four glasses.
CHRISTIAN	Yes, Lord Chancellor.
	(*Exit* CHRISTIAN.)
NICK	Sir Harry, Hugo's got something very interesting he'd like to show you next door.
SIR HARRY	What, in your room?
NICK	No.
HUGO	Yes.
NICK	Yes.
SIR HARRY	What the devil do you want to show me?
HUGO	Er...
NICK	The view.
SIR HARRY	The view?
HUGO	Yes, the view.
NICK	(*opening the connecting door*) Best view in Birmingham.
SIR HARRY	Come on, then. Let's get it over with. Gerald!
GERALD	Yes, Lord Chancellor?
SIR HARRY	Heel!

GERALD   Yes, Lord Chancellor.

(*Exit* SIR HARRY *and* GERALD *to the adjoining room.*)

HUGO   (*sotto voce*) One min max...

(*Exit* HUGO, *following.* NICK *shuts the connecting door and sprints across to the bathroom. He knocks on the door.*)

NICK   Toni.

TONI   (*off*) Has he gone?

NICK   Yes. Quick!

(*Enter* TONI, *dressed.*)

TONI   Ooh, good.

NICK   No, they're all through there. Do as I said. Go and wait in the corridor. When they're safely back here I'll let you in next door. As arranged. Okay?

TONI   Okay. This is rather fun.

(NICK *opens the main door and* TONI *runs out. Enter* SIR HARRY, GERALD *and* HUGO *from the adjoining room.*)

SIR HARRY   What a wonderful view. A veritable vista. A stunning scenic treat. Ten floors of unbroken brickwork overlooking an NCP car park. Have you two gone completely over the edge? (*Knock.*) Ha! That'll be the champagne. Gerald!

GERALD   Yes, Lord Chancellor?

SIR HARRY   Door!

GERALD   Yes, Lord Chancellor.

SIR HARRY   Civil servants!

(GERALD *opens the door. Enter* TONI, *who runs into the room.*)

TONI	I forgot my shoes. (*She almost runs into* SIR HARRY.) Ooh...
SIR HARRY	I say! So this is the little lady you've been hiding from us is it, Hugo?
HUGO	Um...
SIR HARRY	When Gerald told me she was pretty I didn't quite realise...
TONI	(*uncomfortable*) Thank you very much.
SIR HARRY	You old dog!
TONI	I only came in to get my shoes.
NICK	(*fetching* TONI's *shoes*) Off, are you?
TONI	Yes, I think I'd better be off.
SIR HARRY	No. You stay, m'dear. Happy to have you. Nick, you old kill-joy. (*Knock.*) Got to be the blasted champagne this time. Gerald!
GERALD	Yes, Lord Chancellor.
	(GERALD *opens the door. Enter* CHRISTIAN *with champagne and four glasses.*)
CHRISTIAN	Champagne for four, Lord Chancellor.
SIR HARRY	Five! Champagne for five! This is a celebration.
CHRISTIAN	(*setting down the bottle and glasses*) Shall I open it, Lord Chancellor?
SIR HARRY	Yes. What are you waiting for?
CHRISTIAN	Yes, Lord Chancellor.
SIR HARRY	And to think I suspected you might be a touch Australian, Hugo.
HUGO	What? Oh I see. No.

TONI	I really think I ought to be going.
SIR HARRY	I won't hear of it. Have some bubbly, m'dear. (*Handing her a glass.*) Here, get some of that down you.
TONI	Well...
SIR HARRY	Don't be shy.
TONI	Okay.
SIR HARRY	Where are those blasted sandwiches?
GERALD	Gone, Lord Chancellor.
SIR HARRY	Good God, I must have eaten 'em all. (*To* CHRISTIAN.) Young man, more smoked salmon sandwiches. And a fifth glass.
CHRISTIAN	Yes, Lord Chancellor.
	(*Exit* CHRISTIAN.)
SIR HARRY	Come on, Hugo, you're not drinking. Nick. (*He hands them both a glass.*) What's your name, girlie?
TONI	Toni.
SIR HARRY	Toni. Sweet name. Have a top-up, Toni.
TONI	Er... Thanks very much.
SIR HARRY	A toast. To Toni and Hugo!
TONI	Eh? (*Knock.*)
SIR HARRY	That was quick. Gerald!
GERALD	Yes, Lord Chancellor.
	(GERALD *opens the door. Enter* HILARY, *carrying shopping.*)
NICK	Darling!
HILARY	Darling.
SIR HARRY	Hil, old thing.

HILARY	Hello, Daddy.
SIR HARRY	Didn't know you were here.
HILARY	I'm not, actually. Not really. Just popped back to leave my shopping before my arms drop off.
SIR HARRY	She always did know how to spend a man's money, eh, Nick? Ha!
NICK	(*weakly*) Ha!
HILARY	So, Daddy, how's life in the fast lane?
SIR HARRY	Glorious! Whiff of power in the nostrils. Foot on the accelerator of government. Feel forty years younger.
HILARY	Still polishing up that bar of yours?
SIR HARRY	Polish? Clean, you silly moo. "Clean up the Bar!" Eh, Gerald?
GERALD	Yes, Lord Chancellor.
HILARY	Is anyone going to introduce me?
SIR HARRY	This is the albatross, Gerald Blunt.
GERALD	Pleased to meet you, Mrs Willmott.
SIR HARRY	The PM seems to think I need a minder. Can't think why. He's bloody useless. Eh, Gerald?
GERALD	Yes, Lord Chancellor.
SIR HARRY	See what I mean? Ha!
HILARY	(*indicating* TONI) And this is . . . ?
SIR HARRY	Toni. Little friend of Hugo's. Eh, Hugo?
HUGO	Er . . .
TONI	Pleased to meet you, Mrs Willmott.
SIR HARRY	Never thought he had it in him.

HILARY	(*surprised*) Hugo?
HUGO	Yes... Um... Decided this weekend to take the opportunity of inviting along a bit of tot... Tottenham Court Road we met. Solicitors' office. Where she works. Toni. Toni Taylor. And we'll try not to let it interfere with the conference, eh, Toni?
TONI	No.
HUGO	Good.
NICK	Good.
SIR HARRY	Splendid.
TONI	(*suddenly playing the part*) Yes! Ooh, it's brilliant being here. On my weekend. Away from the office. With my Hugo. (*She goes over to him.*) Isn't it, darling?
HUGO	Yes.
TONI	Darling.
HUGO	Darling.
TONI	Mmm.
SIR HARRY	About to propose a toast when you came in, actually, Hil. Grab a glass. Ah, we're two short. Where's that boy? (*Knock.*) Ha! What it is to have power. Eh, Gerald?
GERALD	Yes, Lord Chancellor.
SIR HARRY	Well, open the bloody door, man!
GERALD	Yes, Lord Chancellor.
	(GERALD *opens the door. Enter* CHRISTIAN *with smoked salmon sandwiches and a fifth glass.*)
CHRISTIAN	Your sandwiches, Lord Chancellor.
SIR HARRY	Have you got that glass?
CHRISTIAN	Yes, Lord Chancellor.

SIR HARRY	Good man.
	(CHRISTIAN *hands* SIR HARRY *the glass before going over to* HUGO *with the sandwiches.* SIR HARRY *pours.*)
CHRISTIAN	Would you care for a sandwich, sir?
HUGO	Yes, please.
CHRISTIAN	Proving very popular, if I may say so.
HUGO	Very tasty.
CHRISTIAN	I made them myself.
HUGO	Clever chap.
CHRISTIAN	Very kind of you to say so, sir. Remember, anything you need, don't hesitate to call me.
HUGO	Good lad.
SIR HARRY	There you are, Hil. Get that down you.
CHRISTIAN	Just dial 9 and ask for Christian.
SIR HARRY	Never mind that. Fetch us another glass.
CHRISTIAN	Yes, Lord Chancellor.
GERALD	I don't really need one, Lord Chancellor.
SIR HARRY	Shut up and do as you're told.
GERALD	Yes, Lord Chancellor.
	(*Exit* CHRISTIAN.)
HILARY	He seems like a nice boy . . .
HUGO	Doesn't he? Nick thinks he might be a bit . . . What did you say?
NICK	"Hotel and Catering".
HILARY	Ah.

SIR HARRY	Of course he's hotel and bloody catering. He works here, doesn't he? (NICK *and* HILARY *laugh.*)
HILARY	Daddy!
SIR HARRY	Right, Hugo. Do you want this blasted meeting or don't you?
HUGO	Um...
SIR HARRY	Gerald, put that sandwich down. What do you think this is, a party?
GERALD	No, Lord Chancellor.
SIR HARRY	Can't stay here and disturb the little lady. Mind if we use your room, Hil?
HILARY	Be my guest.
SIR HARRY	Right. We'll go next door, then. Gerald!
GERALD	Lord Chancellor.
SIR HARRY	Come along, Hugo. Take another look at that spectacular view.
	(*Exit* SIR HARRY, HUGO *and* GERALD *to the adjoining room.*)
HILARY	You work for a solicitor then, do you, Toni?
TONI	(*uncomfortable*) Yeah, that's right. Chesney and Fox. In London.
HILARY	And that's how you and Hugo met?
TONI	Mmm.
HILARY	Well. (*Beat.*) Have you known each other long?
TONI	No. Um. Well, not very long. Just quite long. You know.
HILARY	He's one of our oldest friends. Isn't he, darling?

NICK	Who, darling?
HILARY	Hugo, darling.
NICK	Hugo Darling? Oh, Hugo, darling. Yes, very very old. Good old Hugo. (*He drains his glass. Pause.*)
TONI	I don't think I feel very well. Could I be excused?
HILARY	Yes, of course. You know where it is, do you?
TONI	Mmm. (*To herself.*) Eight mins max.
	(*Exit* TONI *to the bathroom.*)
HILARY	Poor girl. She looked green. Do you think she could be pregnant?
NICK	Chance'd be . . . No chance. What? Hugo? Ha! (*Knock.* NICK *answers the door.*)
HILARY	Well, I think it's amazing.
	(*Enter* CHRISTIAN.)
NICK	Ah, Christian.
CHRISTIAN	His Lordship asked for another glass, sir.
NICK	We shan't be needing that now, Christian. In fact, you can clear all this away if you like.
CHRISTIAN	Certainly, sir. (*He starts to clear sandwiches, bottle and glasses.*)
HILARY	Who would have thought it? Hugo! She is a pretty girl, of course, but so young. I shouldn't have thought she was really his sort at all, would you? Far too flighty and up-front. More like the type you used to eye up. (NICK *laughs a little too loudly. Quite matter-of fact:*) I always assumed he was gay, anyway. Well, you know that. I do wish he would open out more. I am terribly fond of him.
CHRISTIAN	Excuse me.

NICK	Christian?
CHRISTIAN	Forgive me, but are you talking about Mister Hugo?
HILARY	Yes.
CHRISTIAN	I'm sure he isn't.
HILARY	Isn't what?
CHRISTIAN	Gay. He can't be. (*Beat.*)
NICK	Thank you, Christian.
CHRISTIAN	Thank you, sir.
	(*Exit* CHRISTIAN.)
HILARY	How come he's so sure?
NICK	Obvious, darling. "Hotel and Catering". They can always tell a bottle from a sauce-pot.
HILARY	Mind you, I've never been completely sure. Or he could be bi-sexual, I suppose. I mean, look at him and Liz.
NICK	Liz?
HILARY	Yes.
NICK	Your sister Liz?
HILARY	Yes.
NICK	Liz and Hugo? Come on.
HILARY	I'm serious. Why do you think she rings up every week?
NICK	To speak to you and the boys. That's not so very odd, is it?
HILARY	Don't be silly. It's not me she rings.
NICK	Yes, it is.
HILARY	Then how come she always ends up talking to you?

NICK	(*joshing*) Obvious, darling. I'm far more interesting than you are.
HILARY	It even crossed my mind that you were having an affair.
NICK	(*laughing*) What? Me and the Judge?
HILARY	Tell me what she talks to you about.
NICK	Oh you know. Chambers. Sir Harry. Hugo.
HILARY	Exactly. Hugo.
NICK	Eh?
HILARY	Nicholas, don't be dim. I reckon she's been in love with Hugo for the past twenty years at least.
NICK	Liz?
HILARY	Yes, darling.
NICK	In love with Hugo?
HILARY	I even wondered whether that's why she moved Chambers all those years ago. Unrequited love. Couldn't bear seeing him every day.
NICK	Blimey. Do you think Hugo knows?
HILARY	I doubt it. Hugo's never the sharpest of men when it comes to affairs of the heart. (*Suddenly thinking.*) Oh I get it.
NICK	What?
HILARY	She's not really his girlfriend at all, is she?
NICK	Who?
HILARY	Trudi, Tracey, Trixie, whatever her name is. The one in the bathroom. You're all in this together, aren't you? The three of you.
NICK	(*increasingly uncomfortable*) What do you mean?
HILARY	You must think I'm very stupid.

NICK	No, I don't.
HILARY	You set this up, didn't you?
NICK	Did I?
HILARY	This whole weekend. You arranged it all.
NICK	Hugo arranged most of it.
HILARY	I didn't know you had it in you, Nicholas. I mean, the nerve. It's brilliant.
NICK	You don't mind?
HILARY	No skin off my nose. But do you think it will work?
NICK	W-work?
HILARY	Will Hugo be able to keep it up?
NICK	I'm sorry, darling, you've lost me.
HILARY	She's obviously a cover for Hugo so that Daddy will think Hugo's a hetero and give him that wretched judgeship.
NICK	Ah.
HILARY	I've always thought Daddy's been completely ridiculous about Hugo. It'll serve him right. Play the homophobic old goat at his own game. Hats off to Hugo!

(*Enter* TONI *from the bathroom.*)

TONI	Ooh, sorry. I don't think I even managed eight mins that time.
HILARY	My husband's told me everything.
TONI	Has he?
HILARY	You've been very clever. I think it's a tremendous idea.
TONI	You mean you don't mind?

HILARY	Why should I mind? It's a stroke of genius. Provided it makes the old man happy.
TONI	You're very broad-minded, aren't you?
HILARY	I don't know about that. I just hope you'll be able to pull it off.
TONI	Pardon?
HILARY	I'm relying on you to make sure he doesn't get cold feet. My advice is, go for it full-throttle.
TONI	Ooh...
HILARY	(*laughing*) Who knows, it could even be the making of him.
TONI	Well, anything I can do to help...
HILARY	It's very decent of you.
TONI	I've never done this sort of thing before, you know.
HILARY	It is a bit unusual, I must admit.
TONI	Well, I'm game, and Nick's game, and – (*Suddenly rather alarmed.*) Are you going to stay?
HILARY	No, I'd just get in the way. Besides, I've got to be off.
NICK	(*looking at his watch*) Have you, darling?
HILARY	Yes, Fiona's expecting me. (*To* TONI.) One of my old girl-friends.
TONI	Ooh...

(*Enter* SIR HARRY, HUGO *and* GERALD *from the adjoining room.*)

SIR HARRY	That's settled, then. A plain, simple introduction from you, Hugo. Got it? Leave the beef to me. They won't know what's hit 'em. Eh, Gerald?
GERALD	No, Lord Chancellor.

SIR HARRY	The speech of a lifetime. Liberals look out! Australians beware! Only the best of British for the Bench. Nick, why aren't you changed?
NICK	Er... We've been chatting. (*He goes to collect his DJ from the closet and makes for the connecting door.*)
SIR HARRY	Chatting? What kind of answer's that? Go and get your kit off, man.
NICK	Right. See you later, darling.
HILARY	Where are you going, darling?
NICK	Next door, darling. I'm taking my clothes in there. To put them on.

(*Exit* NICK.)

SIR HARRY	We at the Bar must set the moral tone. The law must be peopled by people who respect the law.
HILARY	Oh God.

(*Exit* HILARY *to the bathroom.*)

SIR HARRY	Right or wrong. That's the name of the game. We all know what we're talking about. Eh, Gerald?
GERALD	Yes, Lord Chancellor.
SIR HARRY	Disbar any bastard who doesn't measure up. We know who they are. But what we need is evidence, eh, Hugo? Some nice juicy Q C we can name and shame. We'll find 'em.
GERALD	(*looking at his watch*) Excuse me...
SIR HARRY	We'll root 'em out.
GERALD	Lord Chancellor...
SIR HARRY	"Clean up the Bar!"
GERALD	Excuse me...

SIR HARRY	Gerald!
GERALD	Yes, Lord Chancellor?
SIR HARRY	Don't bloody interrupt.
GERALD	Sorry, Lord Chancellor.
HUGO	Don't you think it's time you were getting changed, Sir Harry?
SIR HARRY	What's that?
GERALD	They'll be waiting for you downstairs, Lord Chancellor.
SIR HARRY	Then let 'em wait. Who am I – the Lord Chancellor or what? Ha! (*Knock.*) Gerald!
GERALD	Yes, Lord Chancellor?
SIR HARRY	Door!
GERALD	Yes, Lord Chancellor.
SIR HARRY	Bloody namby-pamby civil servants.

(GERALD *opens the door. There stands* LIZ. *She is a 44-year-old barrister and Circuit Judge, very much the career woman. She is not unattractive, but a little gauche, and she dresses older than her years.*)

HUGO	Liz, hello. Come in.

(*Enter* LIZ.)

LIZ	I'm sorry. I hope I'm not interrupting anything.
SIR HARRY	Not a bit. Just off, actually. Got to go and get changed.
LIZ	Good evening, father.
SIR HARRY	Hello, old thing. See you down there, Hugo. Gerald, come!
GERALD	Yes, Lord Chancellor.

(Exit SIR HARRY *and* GERALD. SIR HARRY *returns immediately.)*

SIR HARRY	*(to* TONI*)* Girlie!
TONI	Yes, Lord... Sir...
SIR HARRY	Come and join us for a snifter.
TONI	Sorry?
SIR HARRY	All right with you, Hugo?
HUGO	Fine by me.
SIR HARRY	Good-oh. Come on.
TONI	Okay.
SIR HARRY	Don't worry, old man. I won't do anything you wouldn't do. Ha!
HUGO	*(weakly)* Ha.
TONI	*(to* SIR HARRY, *as they exit)* Will there be any food?

(Exit SIR HARRY *and* TONI.*)*

LIZ	What was that all about?
HUGO	No idea. So... *(Slight awkward pause.)*
LIZ	I heard you were up here with father, some sort of meeting, and I thought, well, in case there was anything you wished to discuss about tomorrow...
HUGO	No, no...
LIZ	My paper on Children. And I just wanted to say, Hugo, I do so appreciate your asking me to present the paper and lead the discussion...
HUGO	Well, I thought, who better qualified?
LIZ	You're very kind.

(Exit HILARY *from the bathroom.)*

HILARY	Liz.
LIZ	Oh.
HILARY	What are you doing here?
LIZ	Hello, Hilary.
HILARY	Having a little *tête-à-tête* with Hugo?
LIZ	No, no. Purely business. Some of us have to work for a living, you know.
HILARY	I do have a job, Liz, thank you very much.
LIZ	Really?
HILARY	I'm a full-time Family Facilitator.
LIZ	I didn't know.
HILARY	Yes. Minder and housekeeper to Nicholas Willmott Q C and mother to your two Neanderthal nephews.
LIZ	Ah. Sorry. I thought you meant . . . Well, anyway . . . Are you coming down, Hugo?
HUGO	In a minute. I'll just hang on for Nick.
LIZ	Will you be at the dinner, Hilary?
HILARY	No, no. Wives not allowed.
LIZ	See you tomorrow, then. Maybe. Er . . . Right.
	(*Exit* LIZ.)
HILARY	Poor Liz. Goodness, is that the time? I must fly. Fiona'll be wondering. Oh by the way, Hugo. I've spoken to Nick. He's told me all about the girl.
HUGO	Good Lord.
HILARY	I think it's a great idea.
HUGO	You do?

HILARY	Yes. If that's what you two have hatched up I'm quite happy to go along with it.
HUGO	Really?
HILARY	I should have thought that anyone could see that the girl wasn't really your type. Assuming you have a type, that is. No offence meant, Hugo, you know that.
HUGO	None taken. (*Light dawns.*) Oh, I see. You mean Toni and me?
HILARY	Yes. But if you can get one over on father, even if it does mean playing a bit dirty, then I'm all for it.
HUGO	Right.
HILARY	(*chuckling*) But I think you're both very naughty.

(*Enter* NICK *from the adjoining room.*)

NICK	Who invented cuff-links?
HILARY	No idea, darling. But I do know that Fiona hates it if you're late. 'Bye.
NICK	'Bye then, darling. Be good.
HILARY	See you about eleven.
NICK	Have a lovely time.
HILARY	'Bye boys.

(*Exit* HILARY.)

NICK	Where's she gone?
HUGO	Fiona or someone, didn't she say?
NICK	No, you idiot. Toni.
HUGO	Oh. Totty.
NICK	Yes. No. Hugo, behave yourself. Where is she?

HUGO Sir Harry dragged her downstairs for a drink, the poor girl.

NICK Oh God.

HUGO Now look, Nick –

NICK I know what you're going to say, Hugo. I've agreed. She has to go. I'll go downstairs now and prise her away from the old ram.

HUGO That'll look pretty peculiar.

NICK Why?

HUGO She is 'my' girlfriend.

NICK That's true.

HUGO I'd better go.

NICK If you really don't mind.

HUGO I didn't say I didn't mind. (*Knock.*)

TONI (*off*) Nick!

NICK I think she's saved you the trouble.

(HUGO *opens the door. Enter* TONI.)

TONI Ooh, he's terrible, that Lord Sir Harry. He's a groper! And your wife, she's got some very peculiar ideas. Threesomes and foursomes, and things with her friend Fiona and people. I like a bit of fun, but honestly. Ooh, it gives me the willies. I'm off. (*She takes her bag from under the bed.*)

NICK Yes. Probably best.

HUGO That's settled, then. Goodbye, Miss Taylor. Nick, I'll see you down there in a minute.

NICK Right.

HUGO	Just make sure you don't forget that eleven o'clock appointment.
NICK	Understood.
HUGO	Good.
	(*Exit* HUGO.)
TONI	What eleven o'clock appointment?
NICK	Nothing.
TONI	She's coming back, isn't she?
NICK	Who? Hilary?
TONI	And you knew that all the time, didn't you?
NICK	No, I didn't. Not all the time. She wasn't meant to turn up here at all. She was going to be staying at my mother's.
TONI	And what was I supposed to do at eleven o'clock? Turn into a bloody pumpkin?
NICK	I thought you could just go home.
TONI	No I sodding well couldn't just go home! What kind of a girl do you think I am?
NICK	Sorry. No, of course not. I didn't mean that. Look, I'll try and get you a room here if you like.
TONI	Anyway, why did you tell her about us?
NICK	I didn't.
TONI	She said you did.
NICK	No, no. She meant you and Hugo. That's what she thinks.
TONI	So when she said, "Go for it full-throttle", she wasn't saying –

NICK	No. She meant Hugo.
TONI	And she's not into orgies and things?
NICK	(*laughing*) Hilary? No.
TONI	(*softening*) Oh well. That's a bit different, then.
NICK	You mean you'll stay?
TONI	I might.
NICK	(*looking at his watch*) It hardly gives us any time at all.
TONI	You'll have to skip your rotten dinner, then, won't you?
NICK	(*suddenly serious*) Ah, no, sorry. Can't be done.
TONI	Why not?
NICK	Too risky. Hugo would come nosing about looking for me.
TONI	Okay, then. Have the starter. Then say you've got food poisoning or something and come back up. That'll give us a couple of hours.
NICK	You're really still on for it, then?
TONI	I'm not going into Chesney and Fox on Monday morning and tell Sharon and Denise that I was chucked out of the Harcourt Hotel Birmingham on a Saturday night without even so much as a smoked salmon sandwich and a shag.
NICK	I'll order the sandwiches.
TONI	And I'll go and slip into something a bit more comfortable! (*Taking her nightie from her bag.*) Shan't be a tick.
	(*Exit* TONI *to the bathroom.* NICK *dials 9.*)
NICK	Hello, Christian? More sandwiches and a bottle of champagne for Room 101, please. ASAP . . . What's

that? Red roses? No, I don't think so . . . Thank you . . . Yes . . . Thank you, Christian.

(NICK *takes a moment to check his appearance. Some breath-freshener. Enter* TONI *in her nightie, looking a million dollars.*)

TONI Hi.

NICK Hey, look at you!

TONI Go on. Skip the dinner.

NICK No, I told you, that would look fishy. I've got to go down.

TONI Mmm. I'll look forward to that.

NICK You are terrible! (*They kiss. Knock.*) That'll be the champagne.

(NICK *opens the door. Enter* CHRISTIAN *with champagne and two glasses.*)

NICK Christian. Just leave it on the table. I'll deal with it.

CHRISTIAN Certainly, sir.

TONI Oy! Where are my smoked salmon sandwiches?

CHRISTIAN Being prepared as we speak, miss. One round or two?

TONI Ooh, three, I think. I'm starving.

CHRISTIAN Certainly, miss.

(*Exit* CHRISTIAN.)

NICK Come here.

(*They kiss again. Knock. Enter* HUGO *from the adjoining room.*)

HUGO Nick, I just wanted to ask you . . . (*Furious.*) Right. This is the limit. I'm disappointed in you, Nick, I am seriously disappointed. You gave me your word. You promised me faithfully you'd get rid of the girl, and here she is. In your room. In her 'flimsies'.

NICK   But Hugo –

HUGO   Don't you "But Hugo" me. If you want to wreck your marriage, that's your affair, though I think you're a bloody idiot all the same. But this is my reputation we're talking about here.

NICK   Hugo –

HUGO   You can bring yourself down if you want to, but I'm damned if you're going to bring me down with you.

TONI   Here, have some champagne.

HUGO   (*exploding*) I don't want any bloody champagne!

TONI   Come on. (*She hands the bottle to* NICK, *who starts to open it.*) It'll make you feel better.

NICK   Yes, calm down, Hugo. (*The champagne explodes all over* HUGO's *trousers.*)

HUGO   Oh . . . bum!

TONI   Language, Hugo, language.

HUGO   Now look what you've done. I'm soaked!

NICK   Don't get your knickers in a twist, Hugo. It's only champagne.

HUGO   My trousers are ruined.

NICK   (*starting to unbutton*) Here. Have mine.

HUGO   Don't be silly.

NICK   Come on, Hugo. Get 'em off!

HUGO   But there's a lady present.

TONI   Don't worry, Hugo. I'll turn my back.

HUGO	(*starting to unbutton too*) Well, if you're sure you don't mind, old man.
NICK	No. They were coming off anyway. (*He starts taking off his trousers. Knock.*)
TONI	That'll be Christian with my sandwiches.

(*She opens the door.* HUGO *and* NICK *now have their trousers round their ankles. Enter* SIR HARRY.)

SIR HARRY	(*admiringly to* TONI) I say!

(HUGO *and* NICK, *taken unawares, fall over onto the bed in the most compromising of positions.*)

HUGO/NICK	Aaahh!
SIR HARRY	My God!

(HUGO *and* NICK *try to correct their position, but only makes matters worse.*)

HUGO/NICK	Aaahh!
SIR HARRY	My God!

(*Enter* LIZ, *in evening dress.*)

LIZ	Hugo!

(*Enter* CHRISTIAN.)

CHRISTIAN	Smoked salmon sandwiches, anyone?

(*Blackout.*)

ACT TWO

Scene One

Saturday 8.00 PM.

On the bedside table (L) are a bottle of champagne and two glasses, one half-full. TONI, *dressed in her nightie, is standing by the closet, drying her hair. She switches off the hair-dryer. She slips into bed and starts leafing through a hotel magazine. Knock.*

TONI   Enter!

    (*Enter* CHRISTIAN, *wheeling a trolley with* TONI'S *dinner. During the following he hands her a tray and serves boeuf bourguignonne with all the trimmings from silver platters.*)

TONI   Ooh, look at that.

CHRISTIAN   (*expansively, with mock French accent, as he removes the covers*) Madame ordered, I think, the *boeuf bourguignonne*, with *haricots verts* and *pommes de terre* –

TONI   Fab.

CHRISTIAN   (*switching to broad Brummie*) Washed down with a small bottle of *Châteauneuf-du-Pape* '92.

TONI   Ooh . . .

CHRISTIAN   (*back to French*) Would Madame care for a little taste?

TONI   Please. (*He pours. She tastes.*) Oh Christian. It's lovely.

CHRISTIAN   (*normal accent*) I thought you'd like that. (*He pours her half a glass.*)

TONI   This'll be something to tell my grandchildren.

CHRISTIAN   You don't look old enough to be a grandmother.

    (CHRISTIAN *serves the food.*)

TONI	Don't be silly. I didn't mean that. When I'm older I want to have six kids. I love kids.
CHRISTIAN	Do you ever wish you'd had brothers and sisters, then?
TONI	Eh?
CHRISTIAN	Would you like to have had brothers and sisters?
TONI	How did you know – ?
CHRISTIAN	You said you loved kids.
TONI	No, how did you know I'm an only child?
CHRISTIAN	Well, I know it sounds funny, but it's this knack I've got. I've always had it. I only have to meet someone, and nine times out of ten I can tell how many brothers and sisters they've got.
TONI	Really?
CHRISTIAN	And where they come in the family.
TONI	No way!
CHRISTIAN	Sometimes I can even do it with their parents.
TONI	Go on, then. Do my Mum and Dad.
CHRISTIAN	(*looking at her closely*) Er . . . Mother . . . eldest of four.
TONI	Yes!
CHRISTIAN	Father . . . middle of three.
TONI	Yeah, that's right! Blimey. Can you do my friend Sharon?
CHRISTIAN	I could if I met her.
TONI	You've got a real gift, you have. You could be on the telly. Earn a fortune. Does it run in the family? Can your Mum and Dad do it?

CHRISTIAN	I never knew my Mum and Dad.
TONI	Oh.
CHRISTIAN	But I'm sure I'm an only child.
TONI	What happened?
CHRISTIAN	How do you mean?
TONI	To your parents?
CHRISTIAN	No idea. I was brought up in an orphanage.
TONI	(*sadly*) Aaah.
CHRISTIAN	No, it was quite fun, really. I'm sure my parents are still alive. I can feel it in my bones. I even know my mother's name.
TONI	How?
CHRISTIAN	(*producing his birth certificate from his pocket*) It's on my birth certificate. I always carry it with me. Look. "Mother: Elizabeth Smith. Spinster". But I've never been able to trace her.
TONI	And you've no idea who your father was?
CHRISTIAN	No, but . . . This is going to sound silly.
TONI	What?
CHRISTIAN	I can't.
TONI	Go on. You can tell me. (*Beat.*)
CHRISTIAN	You know that lawyer, the tall one?
TONI	Hugo?
CHRISTIAN	I've had this strange feeling about him since the first moment I met him. I feel drawn to him, somehow. I find him completely charismatic.

TONI	(*disbelieving*) Who? Hugo?
CHRISTIAN	Daft, isn't it?
TONI	Not really, no. Not if he's your type.
CHRISTIAN	I don't mean that. (*Beat.*) What I'm trying to say is . . .
TONI	(*encouraging*) Yeah?
CHRISTIAN	It's weird, but . . .
TONI	You think he could be your Dad?
CHRISTIAN	Yes.
TONI	Are you sure?
CHRISTIAN	I think so.
TONI	Ooh, I've gone all goosey. You must tell him.
CHRISTIAN	What if I'm wrong?
TONI	You can't be. You've got the gift.
CHRISTIAN	I'd look bloody stupid.
TONI	You can't just leave it.
CHRISTIAN	What do I say?
TONI	I don't know. Ask him some questions. (*Knock.*)
NICK	(*off*) It's me.
	(*Enter* NICK.)
NICK	It's bloody mayhem down there. Ah, Christian. Make yourself at home, why don't you?
	(CHRISTIAN, *who has made himself comfortable on the bed, gets up.*)
CHRISTIAN	Sorry, sir, I was just . . .

NICK	Never mind. Off you go.
CHRISTIAN	Yes, sir. (*To* TONI, *with French accent.*) I shall return with Madame's dessert in a jiffy.
NICK	Thank you, Christian.
CHRISTIAN	Thank you, sir.
TONI	Christian.
CHRISTIAN	Yes, miss?
TONI	(*crossing her fingers*) Good luck.
CHRISTIAN	Thanks.
	(*Exit* CHRISTIAN.)
NICK	What was that all about?
TONI	Oh just family. He thinks his father may have turned up unexpectedly.
NICK	He's getting a bit forward.
TONI	I like him. I don't fancy him, but I like him. You're nice and early.
NICK	Ah –
TONI	They believed you, then?
NICK	What?
TONI	The food poisoning. Our plan.
NICK	No. That's what I came to tell you. They haven't even started yet. I think Sir Harry's lost his marbles. He's storming around like a buffalo in a bakery, announcing to anyone who'll listen – and it's pretty hard not to – that the Australians are taking over.
TONI	Ooh . . .

NICK	Hugo's in a hell of a state, flapping about in his damp trousers, making frantic efforts at damage limitation, while Sir Harry accuses him of demeaning the office of QC.
TONI	Poor Hugo.
NICK	I'd better get back.
TONI	Can't you stay?
NICK	No. I can't just not be there. They'll come looking for me. I've got to eat the prawn cocktail to get the food poisoning.
TONI	Ooh, I'd kill for a prawn. (*Knock.*)
NICK	Oh God.
	(*He opens the door. Enter* HUGO.)
NICK	Hugo.
HUGO	He's saying things down there that nobody should have to listen to. It's homophobia run riot. He's telling a series of so-called 'Australian' jokes: "I go this way, Hu-go that way!" – accompanied by some very vulgar gestures. I tried to take Gerald aside but he seemed terrified of catching something. The conference is wrecked, my career's in ruins, and for all I know I could even be disbarred, never mind not being made a Judge. I think he's beginning to enjoy himself down there. "Clean up the Bar! Clean up the Bar!" It's like some bloody mantra. You heard what he said about finding a nice juicy Q C to name and shame. Well, he thinks he's found one. You got me into this mess, Nicholas, and you're going to have to get me out of it.
TONI	(*putting her hand up*) Excuse me.
HUGO	Ah, Miss Taylor. Still with us, I see. Splendid.
TONI	I think I'll just pop next door and finish my beef bolognaise. (*No response.*) In there.

(*Exit* TONI, *with her plate, to the adjoining room.*)

HUGO   And another thing.

NICK   What's that?

HUGO   My trousers are still damp.

NICK   I'm sorry, Hugo.

HUGO   So you should be.

NICK   I've said I'm sorry. What more can I do?

HUGO   You can go downstairs and try to prevent that lunatic from wreaking any further havoc. Now!

NICK   Right. All right.

(*Exit* NICK. HUGO *sighs deeply. He feels the discomfort of his damp trousers. He spots the hair-dryer, switches it on and starts drying his trousers. After a few seconds he switches it off, but is still uncomfortable. He puts his hand down his trousers and feels his damp underpants. He unbuttons his trousers, switches on the hair-dryer again and starts drying his underpants. Enter* CHRISTIAN *with a plate of strawberry pavlova. He puts it down and watches* HUGO (*who has his back to him*) *uncertainly.* HUGO *switches off the hair-dryer and turns to find* CHRISTIAN *standing behind him. He jumps.*)

HUGO   Aah!

CHRISTIAN   Good evening, sir.

HUGO   Just having a little, um . . .

CHRISTIAN   Yes, sir?

HUGO   Dry out.

CHRISTIAN   Ah. (*Beat.*) I'm glad I've got you alone, sir.

HUGO   Are you?

CHRISTIAN	At last.
HUGO	Yes?
CHRISTIAN	There are some things I've been wanting to ask you. Certain questions.
HUGO	Mmm?
CHRISTIAN	It's a bit awkward, really.
HUGO	Why's that?
CHRISTIAN	The questions are rather personal.
HUGO	Ah. (*Beat.*) Look, what is this? Some sort of survey?
CHRISTIAN	(*inspired*) Yes. Yes.
HUGO	Fire away, then.
CHRISTIAN	Right. Are you married?
HUGO	No.
CHRISTIAN	Divorced?
HUGO	No.
CHRISTIAN	Single.
HUGO	Yes. (*Beat.*)
CHRISTIAN	Any . . . children at all?
HUGO	No.
CHRISTIAN	Ah.
HUGO	I told you I've never been married.
CHRISTIAN	So, to the best of your knowledge, you definitely haven't fathered a child.
HUGO	No, I told you. I say, what sort of survey is this?

CHRISTIAN	I'm sorry, sir. I have a confession to make. This isn't a survey at all. I'm sorry, but I had to find out.
HUGO	Look, what's all this about?
CHRISTIAN	Just one last thing. Please. And this means a great deal to me. Have you ever had a girlfriend?
HUGO	(*zipping up his trousers*) Good God!
CHRISTIAN	I'm sorry, but it's a question I had to ask.
HUGO	You've been sent up here, haven't you?
CHRISTIAN	What?
HUGO	As a spy.
CHRISTIAN	No.
HUGO	More of this Australian nonsense. I don't believe the depths to which that man will descend. I'm very disappointed in you, Christian.
CHRISTIAN	No, I assure you –
HUGO	Very disappointed indeed. (*Knock.*) I think you'd better leave.
CHRISTIAN	Very well.
HUGO	And you can see who that is on your way out.
CHRISTIAN	Yes, sir.
	(CHRISTIAN *opens the door. Enter* LIZ.)
HUGO	**Liz.**
	(*As soon as possible during the following,* CHRISTIAN *clears the tray and exits with the trolley, leaving the pavlova.*)

LIZ	Hugo, I just had to come up. I can't bear to see you being put through all this – it's too ridiculous. Tell me, how are you? Father's behaving disgracefully. He does talk through his bottom sometimes. I'm sorry, Hugo, but he does. I wish there was something I could do, but he's never valued my judgement. "Clean up the Bar!" What a load of hypocritical old tosh! It'll come back to haunt him, Hugo, you mark my words. Smack on the back of the head like a boomerang. Now that's what I mean by Australian. (*She laughs.*) You don't mind if I help myself to a glass of bubbly, do you? (*She helps herself to the half-full glass.*)
HUGO	I didn't think you drank.
LIZ	I don't, really. Dutch courage.
HUGO	Sorry?
LIZ	(*abruptly, into cross-examination mode*) So, who's the girl?
HUGO	Girl?
LIZ	Yes.
HUGO	What girl?
LIZ	The girl I saw here earlier. The pretty one. When you and Nick had your trousers round your ankles.
HUGO	The pretty one?
LIZ	Yes. Who is she?
HUGO	Um...
LIZ	Is she anything to do with you?
HUGO	No.
LIZ	Look me in the eye, Hugo. Is she your girlfriend?
HUGO	No.

LIZ	Then who is she?
HUGO	She's . . . Toni. Toni Taylor.
LIZ	I don't mean her name, Hugo, and very well you know it. Who is she?
HUGO	She's nothing to do with me.
LIZ	Then what was she doing in your room? In her underwear.
HUGO	It's not my room. It's Nick's room. It's always been Nick's room. But we had to pretend to swop, you see, because he'd brought this girl here for a . . . (*He realises his faux pas.*)
LIZ	Nick?
HUGO	Yes.
LIZ	Nick brought the girl to this hotel for the weekend?
HUGO	Yes.
LIZ	He must be mad.
HUGO	That's what I told him.
LIZ	With Hilary here?
HUGO	Ah, no. She wasn't supposed to be, you see. She was spending the weekend with her mother-in-law.
LIZ	Who? Moaning Morag?
HUGO	You won't say anything, will you? To Hilary, I mean.
LIZ	Where's this Toni creature now?
HUGO	She's . . . No idea. Gone. Probably.
LIZ	Well, I think Hilary should be told.
HUGO	No. Nothing happened. I can vouch for that.

LIZ	Are you sure?
HUGO	Absolutely.
LIZ	Well, I don't know. Did Hilary see her?
HUGO	Yes, but only briefly.
LIZ	My sister's no fool, you know. She'll wonder. What if she asks?
HUGO	(*as if inspired*) I know! We could say she was with me. My girlfriend.
LIZ	Your girlfriend? She'd never buy that.
HUGO	You nearly did. And you're no fool.
LIZ	All right, Hugo. Since you're sure nothing happened. I suppose there's no point in causing Hilary unnecessary pain and distress. Your girlfriend! (*She laughs.*) I think you're very clever, Hugo, to think of that.
HUGO	Thank you.
LIZ	(*draining her glass*) Now, I'm going downstairs to persuade that idiotic father of mine to come up here and have a sensible talk with you. That's what I'm going to do. Well done, Hugo. (*She kisses* HUGO *on the cheek.*)
HUGO	Oh.
	(*Exit* LIZ, *leaving her glass on the bedside table.*)
HUGO	That was nice. (*Pacing up and down, he rehearses what he'll say to* SIR HARRY. *Firmly:*) Listen, Sir Harry ... No, too strong (*Pleadingly:*) Please, Sir Harry ... No, no. Too weak. (*Aggressively:*) Now look here, Lumsden-Clark ... I don't think so. (*He notices the strawberry pavlova.*) Ah! (*He picks it up, and a spoon. Reasonably:*) I say, Sir Harry ... (*Satisfied.*) Mmm. (*He is about to help himself to the pavlova.*)
	(*Enter* TONI *from the adjoining room.*)

TONI	Oy! That's my strawberry pavlova.
HUGO	Is it? Sorry.
TONI	(*taking it*) Cheeky thing.
	(*Exit* TONI *to the adjoining room.*)
HUGO	(*reasonably*) I say, Sir Harry ... (*Knock.*) Sir Harry! (*He opens the door.*)
	(*Enter* HILARY.)
HILARY	Hugo? What are you doing here?
	(*During the following,* HILARY *searches the room, the bathroom and the closet – but she doesn't look under the bed.*)
HUGO	I thought you were Sir Harry.
HILARY	Why?
HUGO	Well, I thought he was coming up. You see, I couldn't go down because he's not speaking to me. So Nick went down first, then Liz came up and said she'd go back down and send him up to me. So that's who I thought you were.
HILARY	Hugo, what are you talking about?
HUGO	Sir Harry's got it into his head that Nick and I are having some sort of gay tangle.
HILARY	(*laughing*) Nick?
HUGO	All a ridiculous misunderstanding, of course. But you know what your father's like when he gets a bee in his bonnet.
HILARY	What are you doing in here, Hugo?
HUGO	Totally absurd. What?

HILARY	Why aren't you in your own room?
HUGO	Ah. Good question.
HILARY	Where's Nick?
HUGO	Downstairs. I told you.
HILARY	(*having finished her search*) And where's that girl? Is she still here?
HUGO	No. She's next door. She's eating strawberry pavlova.
HILARY	(*beginning to be satisfied*) She is still here, and she's in your room.
HUGO	Absolutely.
HILARY	So she is with you?
HUGO	Yes.
HILARY	Just clarify this for me, would you, Hugo. She is a cover, isn't she?
HUGO	What?
HILARY	A cover. The girl.
HUGO	A cover-girl? No, I don't think so. She could be. She is very pretty.
HILARY	No, Hugo. Listen to me. She's not a real girlfriend, is she?
HUGO	Definitely. Yes. Very real.
HILARY	Your girlfriend.
HUGO	Yes. Yes.
HILARY	(*still doubtful*) Mmm. Thank you, Hugo. (*Knock.*)
HUGO	That will be Sir Harry.

(HUGO *opens the door. Enter* LIZ.)

HUGO Liz.

LIZ He says you've got to go down, Hugo. He won't come up. He's holding court. Going from bad to worse. "Q C", according to him, now stands for "Queer as a Coot". (HILARY *laughs.*) It's not funny, Hilary. Father's making a real ass of himself.

HILARY Tell me something new.

LIZ Please. Do go, Hugo.

HUGO If you really think it will do any good. Oh God . . .

(*Exit* HUGO.)

HILARY I'm having a glass of champagne. Will you join me?

LIZ No, I don't think so.

HILARY (*pouring herself a glass*) Sure?

LIZ Not for me, really. I should be getting along.

HILARY Hold on a moment. There's something I want to ask you. Do you mind?

LIZ Why should I mind?

HILARY When I was here earlier I met this girl. Toni. Who everyone said was a girlfriend of Hugo's. Well, she was very young and extremely attractive. It didn't seem quite right, somehow. Then I realised she must be a cover for Hugo – I mean, not really his girlfriend, but so that he'd come across as better judge material to Daddy. Future family man and all that rubbish. Then, over supper with my friend Fiona, in Moseley, as I was describing it all, having a bit of a laugh actually, it began to seem so terribly unlikely. I suddenly had this awful feeling of unease. Now Hugo's told me that she really is his girlfriend. But I still don't quite believe it somehow. Liz, what I want to ask you is this. Have you noticed Nick behaving strangely at all?

LIZ	No more than usual.
HILARY	Liz, I'm serious.
LIZ	Sorry. Listen, Hil. The girl is with Hugo. It's a fact.
HILARY	How do you know?
LIZ	He told me so himself.
HILARY	He told you too?
LIZ	Off his own bat. Completely independently.
HILARY	Amazing. (*Beat.*) Oh, Liz. Forgive me. I am sorry.
LIZ	Why?
HILARY	You must be so upset.
LIZ	Why should I be upset?
HILARY	Well, I thought . . . Didn't you and Hugo . . . ? You know. Didn't you once . . . ?
LIZ	(*realising that she should be upset by* HUGO's *infidelity*) Oh. Yes, I am rather upset, actually. In fact, I'm very upset. (*Getting tearful.*) I'm sorry, Hil. I'm sorry!
HILARY	Why don't you have that drink?
LIZ	(*sobbing*) Yes. Give me a drink. I need a drink.
HILARY	Calm down, Liz. (*Handing* LIZ *a glass of champagne.*) Calm down. Hil's here.
LIZ	(*downing the glass in one*) Better now.
HILARY	All right? Really?
LIZ	(*recovering*) Yes, I'm fine. It was over twenty years ago, anyway. You can't hold a candle for someone for ever. Hugo's entitled to his own life, and if he's found

himself a girlfriend – even if she is less than half his age – who am I to get upset about it? I'm just a silly old sausage. I'll go down and leave you in peace. (*Knock.*)

HILARY Now what?

(HILARY *opens the door. Enter* HUGO. *He is very fraught.*)

HUGO It's quite hopeless. He still refuses to speak to me.

LIZ But he said he wanted to see you.

HUGO (*a little sharply*) Well, he appears to have changed his mind, doesn't he?

HILARY Look, you two –

HUGO No idea what he's on about half the time.

HILARY I don't wish to appear rude –

HUGO He's talking about beach boys with bum bags and bum boys with beach balls. I don't know.

HILARY But I really have had one hell of a day.

LIZ Can't Nick do anything?

HUGO Nick? He's no help at all. Besides, Sir Harry won't let me anywhere near him.

HILARY I think I'll slip into something more comfortable –

HUGO Says I've corrupted him.

LIZ Oh Hugo.

HILARY (*pointedly*) And settle in for an early night.

HUGO Sorry?

HILARY Provided that's all right with you two, of course.

(*Exit* HILARY *to the closet.*)

LIZ	Oh dear. I think she's upset.
HUGO	Not half as upset as I am.
	(*Enter* TONI *from the adjoining room.*)
TONI	(*stopping in her tracks*) Ooh . . . Hello . . . Sorry, Hugo. I thought you'd be on your own. (*Uncertain of the role she's supposed to be playing.*) Er . . . darling. (*Little wave.*) See you in a min.
LIZ	Hugo!
HUGO	What?
LIZ	You . . . beast! (*She slaps* HUGO's *face.*)
TONI	Ooh . . .
	(*Exit* TONI *to the adjoining room.*)
LIZ	You told me she had nothing to do with you. How could you lie to me, Hugo? She was in your room all the time.
	(*Enter* HILARY *from the closet, in her dressing gown.*)
LIZ	Oh Hugo!
	(*Exit* LIZ.)
HILARY	Liz? Hugo, what's going on. (*She opens the door and calls out.*) Liz!
	(*Re-enter* LIZ. *She grabs the bottle of champagne.*)
LIZ	You . . . animal!
	(*Exit* LIZ.)
HILARY	What was that all about? (HUGO *is speechless.*) Hugo? Have you done something to upset her?

HUGO	Oh dear. I think I'd better go and see if she's all right. Do you mind?
HILARY	No, Hugo. You go.

(*Exit* HUGO. HILARY *exits to the bathroom. Enter* TONI, *cautiously, with her glass. Now the room is hers again she relaxes and goes to pour herself some more champagne. She sees the bottle has gone and dials 9.*)

TONI	Hello? Christian? . . . (*Putting on a Brummie accent.*) My mother was the eldest of four, my father was the middle of three – who am I? . . . Correct! Ooh, I said you should be on the telly. (*Normal accent.*) Now, Christian, seriously. I need another bottle of bubbly . . . No, I've hardly had a look in . . . Yeah, all right, the most expensive. The lawyers are paying . . . (*Laughing.*) I know. That's what my Mum says . . . What? Red roses? Yeah, why not? (*She puts down the phone, slips into bed and starts reading her magazine. Knock.*)
NICK	(*off*) It's only me.

(*Enter* NICK.)

TONI	Hi!
NICK	They've started at last. I slipped away as soon as I could. (*He mimes exaggerated vomiting.*)
TONI	You all right?
NICK	No. (*He sits on the bed*) That's what I did. It worked.
TONI	You're ever so good. (*Beat.*) Come on, then.
NICK	What?
TONI	Aren't you going to get undressed?
NICK	(*not moving*) You bet.
TONI	We haven't got long.
NICK	No. Right. Yes.

(He starts undressing. He will strip down to his vest, underpants and socks. He lays his DJ over a chair.)

TONI   You know Hugo?

NICK   Yes, I know Hugo.

TONI   He was here with that funny woman.

NICK   Who? Liz?

TONI   I think he must have upset her. She slapped his face and everything. It was terrible. And he was very, very naughty. You know what he tried to do?

NICK   What?

TONI   I came in just in time to stop him doing it.

NICK   Doing what?

TONI   Eating my strawberry pavlova.

NICK   That's terrible.

TONI   Yeah, I know. (NICK *slips the bolt on the adjoining door.*)

NICK   No more Hugos.

TONI   No more Hugos. (NICK *gets into bed.*)

NICK   Well...

TONI   At last.

NICK   Yes...

(They are about to embrace when HILARY *enters from the bathroom.)*

HILARY   (*peering*) Darling, is that you?

(Toni *slips down under the duvet and* Nick *leans nonchalantly over her.*)

NICK (*expansive*) Darling!

HILARY Thank God for that. I wasn't sure for a minute. I've just taken my lenses out. What are you doing in bed?

NICK Food poisoning.

HILARY What? Hang on, I've got my earplugs in. (*She takes them out.*)

NICK Food poisoning. Terrible. Must have been a dodgy prawn.

HILARY (*sitting on the bed*) You poor darling. You know what Auntie Meryl always says: "Never trust a prawn, an oyster or a winkle".

NICK I didn't expect you back so early.

HILARY I've had the most ghastly evening with Fiona. You were quite right about her. She's a cow. Spent the whole time slagging you off. I couldn't bear it. So I left. Move over. What are you doing on my side?

NICK (*making it clear to* TONI) Move over. Right.

(*He moves over to make room for* HILARY. TONI *falls out the other side onto the floor with a bump.*)

HILARY What was that?

NICK No idea. (*Knock.*) Ah. Must have been the door. Someone at the door. (TONI *rolls under the bed, but her feet stick out at the end. Calling:*) Who is it?

CHRISTIAN (*off*) It's Christian.

NICK Ah, Christian. Come in.

(*Enter* CHRISTIAN.)

CHRISTIAN	(*French accent*) Champagne and two dozen red roses for the only child of the eldest of four and the middle of three.
HILARY	Whatever are you talking about?
CHRISTIAN	Oh. (*Looking* NICK *straight in the eye. Normal accent.*) Sorry, sir. Have I got the wrong room?
NICK	Er . . . (*Suddenly expansive.*) No, no. Certainly not. Bring them in!

(CHRISTIAN *puts the roses and the champagne on the downstage table.*)

HILARY	Oh darling! You've never remembered the date before.
NICK	Date?
CHRISTIAN	Your birthday, madam?
HILARY	No, it's our wedding anniversary.
CHRISTIAN	Indeed, madam? May I offer you my congratulations?
NICK	Thank you, Christian.
HILARY	And two dozen red roses. Darling, how clever of you to get the number just right.
CHRISTIAN	Twenty-four years. That's quite a feat. (*He notices* TONI's *feet. Warning:*) Feet!

(TONI *withdraws her feet.*)

HILARY	You really shouldn't have, darling. You're too, too sweet. (*Yawn.*) What a pity I've just taken my sleeping pill.

(NICK *and* CHRISTIAN *exchange looks as* HILARY *yawns again and sinks down onto her pillow.*)

Scene Two

Ten minutes later.

NICK is sitting up in bed. HILARY is lying beside him, apparently asleep. TONI is still under the bed.

HILARY	(*forcing herself up*) I'm trying, darling. (*Big yawn.*) I really am trying.
NICK	I know you are, darling.
HILARY	(*falling back*) I think I'm going.
NICK	Well, if you've got to go, you've got to go.
HILARY	(*sitting up again*) Thank you for the roses, my sweet.
	(*She yawns again and this time falls asleep. Pause. NICK studies HILARY to make sure she's asleep.*)
TONI	Is she asleep?
NICK	Shh . . .
TONI	Sorry, but . . .
NICK	(*louder*) Shhh!
HILARY	Mmm . . . ?
NICK	Darling? (*Silence. To TONI, whispering.*) It's all right. You can come out.
TONI	(*emerging*) Blimey. I've been under there for ages.
NICK	Only ten minutes.
TONI	I know, but nine mins max.
NICK	Sorry.
TONI	Ooh, I'm freezing.
NICK	Come on, then. Cuddle up. (*Light snore from HILARY.*)

TONI	We can't! Not here.
NICK	We could go to Hugo's room.
TONI	What if he comes back?
NICK	He won't. Not for ages. I know these dinners. He won't be up till gone midnight. We've got hours.
TONI	I don't know...
NICK	I'll just check he's not there if you like.
TONI	Nick...

(*Exit* NICK *to the adjoining room.*)

NICK	(*putting his head round the door*) All clear.
HILARY	(*stirring*) Darling...
TONI	Ooh...

(*Exit* TONI, *shutting the connecting door behind her.* HILARY, *murmuring in her sleep – "Ooh, darling!" – and unsteady on her feet, gets up and exits to the bathroom.*)

HUGO	(*off, loudly*) Just what the hell do you think you think you are doing?

(*Enter* HUGO *from the adjoining room, followed by* NICK.)

NICK	Hugo...
HUGO	It's time for Hilary to be told.
NICK	Shh, Hugo! You'll wake her up.

(*Enter* TONI, *who hovers by the connecting door.*)

HUGO	Too damned right I'll wake her up. Hilary!
TONI	Ooh...

HUGO	(*looking for her under the duvet*) Where's she gone?
NICK	Er . . . No idea, old man.
HUGO	This deception has gone on long enough. God knows how many times you said you'd get rid of the girl. Hilary must be told. It's only fair.
NICK	You're serious, aren't you?
HUGO	I am deadly serious.

(*Enter* HILARY *from the bathroom, still sleep-walking.*)

HILARY	(*in her sleep*) Sweetums.
HUGO	Ah.
TONI	Ooh . . .

(*Exit* TONI *to the adjoining room.*)

HILARY	(*in her sleep*) Darling . . .
HUGO	Hilary.

(HILARY, *about to get into bed, stops and stands in front of* HUGO, *apparently listening to him.*)

HILARY	(*in her sleep*) Mmm?
HUGO	I have something very important to say to you. I want you to listen carefully. Are you listening? Carefully?
HILARY	(*in her sleep*) Mmm.
HUGO	Good. I'm sorry to have to tell you this, but Nick –
HILARY	(*in her sleep*) Darling . . .
HUGO	Your husband –
HILARY	(*in her sleep*) Four and twenty . . .
HUGO	Hilary?

HILARY	(*in her sleep*) Baked in a pie. (*She gets into bed.*)
HUGO	What?
HILARY	(*in her sleep*) Very, very sweet.
HUGO	Nick –
HILARY	(*in her sleep*) Nighty, nighty.
NICK	(*weakly*) Pyjama, pyjama. (HILARY *falls back onto her pillow.*)
HUGO	You can't fall asleep on me now, Hilary. This is very important. (*Beat.*) I say, old thing, are you all right? (*He tries to lift her up, but she is as limp as a rag doll.*)
	(*Enter* TONI *from the adjoining room.*)
HUGO	I can't wake her up. My God. Do you think she's taken an overdose? She must have found out. (*Desperately trying to revive her.*) Wake up, Hillers! Wake up!
NICK	Shh, Hugo.
HUGO	(*shaking* HILARY) Don't go to sleep!
TONI	Stop him, Nick.
HUGO	Call an ambulance.
NICK	Hugo, no . . .
HUGO	My God. You don't care, do you? I knew you were cheating on the poor woman, but I didn't realise quite how contemptuous you were of her welfare.
TONI	Shh, Hugo. She'll wake up.
HUGO	We want her to wake up, you callous harpy.
TONI	No, we don't.
HUGO	What do you mean, you don't? My God, you're in this together.

NICK	No, Hugo, listen –
HUGO	It's a conspiracy.
TONI	It isn't.
HUGO	Murder most foul!
NICK	She's taken a sleeping tablet, Hugo.
HUGO	What?
NICK	One sleeping tablet.
HILARY	(*in her sleep*) Murder most foul.
HUGO	Then we'll have to wake her up. Coffee. We'll give her coffee. (*He picks up the receiver.*) I'm still going to tell her.
TONI	Ooh . . .
	(HUGO *dials 9. He gets increasingly exasperated during the course of his conversation with* CHRISTIAN.)
HUGO	You're not getting off that lightly. Ah, Christian. Hugo Barnes, Room 101 . . . No, I'm next door . . . I'm very well, thank you. Now, Christian . . . Engaged? I don't really see . . . Look here, what is this – another bloody survey? . . . No, I told you, no children at all. Of any kind . . . What?
TONI	This isn't going to work, Nicholas.
HUGO	Dry cleaning?
NICK	No, I've got an idea.
HUGO	Yes, yes, I'll tell him.
TONI	It's my fault. I should never have come.
NICK	Toni, please . . .
HUGO	Look, will you stop wittering and listen to me!

HILARY	(*in her sleep*) I'm all ears, darling.
TONI	Let's face it, what we're doing is wrong.
HUGO	Good. Coffee. Strong and black. Quick as you can. (*He slams the phone down.*)
NICK	What did he mean, dry cleaning?
HUGO	(*shouting: he has nearly lost his rag*) If you want your dinner jacket cleaned, leave it over the chair, he'll collect it and it will be done overnight.
NICK	(*calmly*) All right, Hugo. Understood. (*Knock.*)
HUGO	Golly, that was quick.

(HUGO *opens the door. Enter* GERALD. *He doesn't notice* HILARY.)

HUGO	Gerald?
TONI	Ooh . . .

(*Exit* TONI *to the adjoining room.*)

GERALD	Gentlemen. Forgive the invasion of your privacy at this indelicate hour, but I am instructed by the Lord Chancellor –
HUGO	To check up on us, eh, Gerald?
GERALD	I wouldn't go as far as to say that, sir.
HUGO	Oh wouldn't you, Gerald? Then how far would you go? As far as your sexually-obsessed superior thinks I've gone with Mr Willmott, standing there as he is in his very fetching underpants, eh, Gerald? Eh, eh, eh?
GERALD	I only came –
HUGO	To see if you could dig up any further irrefutable evidence of Australian activity, eh, Gerald? (*Furious,*

grabbing GERALD *by the lapels.*) Well, you can tell your barmy boss from me and you can tell him straight, the homophobic old goat: he can take his judgeship and he can stick it where the sun never shines. It was a bum job anyway. I've decided to emigrate. To Australia. I'm applying for positions in Sydney. Whoever he may be. (*Beat.*) Well, go on, man. What the hell are you waiting for?

GERALD (*shocked*) Yes, sir.

(*Exit* GERALD.)

NICK Well done, Hugo. That was subtle. Now you've really queered your pitch.

HUGO Thank you so much for that sensitive choice of words.

(*Enter* TONI *from the adjoining room.*)

TONI Nick...

HUGO I'm absolutely knackered. I'm going to bed.

NICK Good idea.

HUGO And you're coming with me.

NICK Am I?

HUGO We've been charged. We may as well provide the evidence.

NICK Good Lord!

HUGO Twin beds, Nick. Don't be silly.

NICK Where's Toni going to sleep?

HUGO Not with us, that's for sure.

TONI It's all right. Nick's arranged a room. Haven't you?

NICK Er...

TONI	(*cross*) I don't believe this. You said.
HILARY	(*in her sleep*) I don't believe this.
TONI	Ooh . . .
HILARY	(*in her sleep*) You said.
HUGO	Come on.

(*Exit* HUGO *to the adjoining room, dragging* NICK *with him.*)

NICK	(*over his shoulder*) See you later.

(*Exit* NICK. *We hear the door bolted from the other side.*)

HILARY	(*in her sleep*) See you later, darling.
TONI	Ooh . . . (*She tries the adjoining door.*) Ooh . . .

(*She looks lost for a moment, then goes to the main door as if to leave. She realises that she isn't dressed. She goes round to the far side of the bed, fetches her bag from underneath and takes it to the closet. The phone rings. She returns from the closet without the bag. She hesitates.*)

HILARY	(*in her sleep*) It's for you-hoo!
TONI	Ooh . . . (*She crosses to answer the phone. Very quietly:*) Hello? . . . (*Louder:*) Yes, it's me. Who's that? . . . Ooh, hello my Lordship . . . No, he's gone. He's not here . . . Yes, I'm on my own. Except – (SIR HARRY *has hung up.*) Hello? . . . Hello? . . . Ooh . . .

(*She puts the phone down. She crosses back round to the closet but, before she goes in,* HILARY *speaks.*)

HILARY	(*in her sleep*) Was it for me, darling?
TONI	(*deep voice*) No, darling.
HILARY	(*in her sleep*) All right. I'll take it in the study.

TONI   Ooh . . .

             (*She suddenly needs to go to the loo. She is about to go to the bathroom when there is a knock at the door.*)

TONI   Ooh . . .

             (*A snore from* HILARY. *A second knock.*)

TONI   Ooh . . .

             (*She decides to answer the door. Enter* SIR HARRY, *dressed in his DJ.*)

SIR HARRY   Hello, girlie!

TONI   (*whispering and nervous*) Hello.

SIR HARRY   All alone, eh?

TONI   (*whispering*) Yes.

SIR HARRY   Where's Hugo?

TONI   (*whispering*) The boys are next door. They've gone to bed and locked the door.

SIR HARRY   Humph. Bloody antipodeans! So, that leaves a clear field, eh?

TONI   Mmm?

SIR HARRY   (*whispering*) I must say, that's a very becoming little number.

TONI   (*whispering*) Is it?

SIR HARRY   (*whispering*) Why are we whispering?

TONI   (*whispering*) I don't know, really. (*Floundering.*) Er . . . More romantic?

SIR HARRY   I see we're speaking the same lingo.

TONI	I think I need to go to the bathroom.
SIR HARRY	Freshen up, eh?
TONI	Mmm.
SIR HARRY	Well, don't be long. I'll be waiting.
TONI	Yes. (*Ironic.*) I'll look forward to that.

(*Exit* TONI *to the bathroom.*)

SIR HARRY	(*with relish*) I say!

(*A snore from* HILARY. SIR HARRY *is briefly puzzled, but dismisses the noise and quickly undresses down to his vest and long-johns. He places his DJ over the chair. Knock.*)

SIR HARRY	Come! (*Another knock*) Oh for Heaven's sake . . .

(*He opens the door. Enter* GERALD.)

SIR HARRY	Gerald. What the devil do you want?
GERALD	I considered it imperative to communicate with you, Lord Chancellor. Precipitately.
SIR HARRY	Ever thought of speaking plain English, Gerald?
GERALD	I beg your pardon, Lord Chancellor?
SIR HARRY	Oh never mind. Just come in and shut the door.
GERALD	Yes, Lord Chancellor.
SIR HARRY	What the hell are you doing here, anyway?
GERALD	They're asking for you downstairs, Lord Chancellor.
SIR HARRY	Tell them I'm otherwise engaged. (HILARY *sits up in bed.*)
HILARY	(*in her sleep*) Darling.

SIR HARRY   Eh?

HILARY   (*in her sleep*) Sweetums.

SIR HARRY   Hilary?

HILARY   (*in her sleep*) Come to bed.

SIR HARRY   Good God!

HILARY   (*in her sleep, seductively*) It is Saturday night.

SIR HARRY   Ah. (*Beat.*) Er . . . Believe you've met my daughter.

GERALD   Yes, Lord Chancellor.

(*Exit* GERALD. HILARY, *still asleep, starts humming "The Last Waltz".*)

SIR HARRY   Hil? Hil, old thing, are you all right? (*He tries to rouse her.*) Hil?

(*There is a knock on the connecting door.* SIR HARRY *slips into the closet. The door opens slightly.* NICK'S *head appears.*)

NICK   Toni. All clear.

(*Enter* NICK, *leaving the connecting door wide open. He crosses to the bathroom and taps quietly on the door.*)

TONI   (*off, nervously*) I'll be a few more minutes.

(*A loud snore from* HILARY. NICK *gets* HILARY *out of bed and steers her into* HUGO'S *room. As she resumes her singing of "The Last Waltz" this becomes a dance. Exit* NICK *with* HILARY. *Enter* CHRISTIAN, *with cafetière of coffee, cup and sugar bowl. He sets the tray on the table. He tidies the bed, closes the connecting door and takes the two DJs away for cleaning. Exit* CHRISTIAN. *Enter* SIR HARRY *from the closet. He looks for* HILARY *under the duvet.*)

SIR HARRY	Hil? Hil, old thing? . . . Humph! (*He crosses to the chair and sees that his DJ has disappeared.*) Hilary? (*Beat.*) All right, a joke's a joke. Stop playing silly buggers . . .

(*He looks for her under the bed – L. Enter* NICK *from the adjoining room.* SIR HARRY *stands up.*)

BOTH	(*jumping*) Ah!
NICK	Sir Harry! What are you doing here?
SIR HARRY	Looking for your wife
NICK	My wife?
SIR HARRY	Yes. She was here a moment ago.
NICK	Was she?
SIR HARRY	But she seems to have disappeared.
NICK	Really?
SIR HARRY	You don't seem very concerned.
NICK	Well . . .
SIR HARRY	I tell you, man, she's disappeared.
NICK	She's probably just gone for a walk.
SIR HARRY	In her jim-jams? At this time of night? Don't be a bloody fool. (*He opens the main door and calls out.*) Hilary! (*He closes the door and dials 0.*)
NICK	What are you doing?
SIR HARRY	Hello? Reception? . . . I want to report a missing person . . . Room 101 . . . Well, she's not in Room 101 because she's missing, isn't she? . . . She was in Room 101 . . . If I knew where she was now I wouldn't be reporting her missing, would I, you bumbling oaf . . . Well, bloody well look for her! (*He slams down the receiver.*) What was she doing in Hugo's bed, anyway?

NICK   Er...

SIR HARRY   Trying to reform him or something?

NICK   Um...

SIR HARRY   Bloody Australians!

NICK   Come to that, what are you doing here? In your underwear?

SIR HARRY   Ah, now, well. I've got a little thing going tonight, as a matter of fact. She's in the bathroom now. Freshening up. (*Knocking on the bathroom door.*) How are you doing in there, girlie?

TONI   (*off*) One more minute.

NICK   You're wasting your time on that one, I'm afraid.

SIR HARRY   (*with relish*) I don't think so.

NICK   You've heard of Australians. Well, she's a bit – how shall I put it? – Tasmanian.

SIR HARRY   Not with you, old man.

NICK   (*prompting*) Australian? Tasmanian?

SIR HARRY   My God, you mean...? I don't believe it. She was here, in her little slip. She was mad for it. Hilary was here too. In bed. (*Sudden realisation.*) Good Lord alive! You're all in this together, aren't you? You two next door, these two – what do you call 'em? – Tasmanians here. Bed-swopping, room-swapping, sex-swapping. Is there no morality? (*The phone rings.*) That was quick. They must have found her. (*He answers the phone.*) Hello... (*Disguising his voice.*) No. Sorry. Wrong number. (*He puts down the receiver.*)

NICK   Who was that?

SIR HARRY   Liz. Sounded half-sozzled. Didn't want her knowing I was here. Look at me. Can you imagine? (*The phone rings again.* SIR HARRY *picks it up and puts his hand*

	over the receiver.) It's her again. You take it. (*He hands the receiver to* NICK.)
NICK	Liz?... No, it's Nick... No, she's... er... just popped out.
SIR HARRY	(*looking for his DJ*) Where's the bloody thing gone?
NICK	(*to* LIZ) It's all right, calm down...
SIR HARRY	No, I bloody well won't calm down.
NICK	Hugo?
SIR HARRY	Have you seen it?
NICK	(*to* SIR HARRY) No. (*To* LIZ.) No. I mean, yes. Yes, of course you can... Liz...? (*He puts the receiver down.*) She's coming round.
SIR HARRY	What the devil for?
NICK	I don't know. She sounded distraught. Something about Hugo.
SIR HARRY	You'll have to get rid of her. That girlie will be out any second. I have my reputation to consider, you know.
NICK	Quite. (*Knock.*) You'd better hide in the closet.
LIZ	(*off*) Nick?
NICK	I'll talk to her.
SIR HARRY	Stout fellow.
	(*Exit* SIR HARRY *to the closet.* NICK *opens the door. Enter* LIZ, *rather the worse for wear.*)
NICK	Liz.
LIZ	Nick, I'm sorry for disturbing you, with your funny tummy and everything, but I simply had to talk to someone. Is Hilary back?

NICK   Er...

LIZ   I can trust you, can't I? I'm at the end of my tether. Father's livid. Poor, darling Hugo. His career's in tatters. I have a plan. Will you help me, Nick?

NICK   Um...

LIZ   What a darling you are. Now, listen. Father must see for himself that Hugo isn't one of these – what does he call them? – Australians. Oh it's all so stupid and unnecessary. But what if he were to see Hugo in bed with the girl?

NICK   What?

LIZ   I can't get direct access to Hugo's room, so I'll have to use your connecting door. You don't mind, do you? Father need only have a little peep. Hugo won't know anything about it if we're clever. What do you think?

NICK   I think it's a dreadful idea.

LIZ   Do you?

NICK   Impossible. And quite immoral. It's a betrayal of Hugo's privacy. An infringement of his civil liberties. Moreover, it's a gross breach of the European Convention of Human Rights. I'm surprised at you, Liz.

LIZ   (*wailing*) What about my human rights?

NICK   Don't you think you've got this a wee bit out of perspective? Hugo would be very cross if he thought we were spying on him.

LIZ   You're right, Nick. You're absolutely right. It was silly of me. But I just wanted to do something. You do see that, don't you?

NICK   Of course.

LIZ   Thank you, Nick. You're a good friend.

(*The connecting door opens. Enter* HUGO, *in striped pyjamas.*)

HUGO Right, you utter bastard. I know what you're up to. (*Seeing* LIZ.) Liz. (*Warily.*) What are you doing here?

LIZ Oh Hugo. I only came to help.

HUGO Help? Help who?

LIZ Hugo . . .

(*Enter* TONI *from the bathroom.*)

TONI Ooh, I couldn't stay in there a minute longer. (*Looking round.*) Oh good, he's gone.

(*Enter* HILARY, *still asleep, from the adjoining room. She makes straight for* HUGO *and embraces him.*)

HILARY (*in her sleep*) Good night, darling. You were wonderful. (*She gets into bed.*)

LIZ Hugo!

HUGO Yes?

HILARY (*in her sleep*) Sexy beast.

LIZ You . . . bastard! (*She slaps* HUGO's *face.*)

HILARY (*in her sleep*) Bastard.

(*Exit* LIZ.)

TONI Oh Hugo. Have you been a naughty boy?

HUGO Don't be silly.

NICK Toni, I'm ever so sorry about all this. But I think you really had better be on your way.

TONI Suits me. What's my room number?

NICK I told you, I haven't –

TONI	I know.
NICK	I didn't manage –
TONI	You didn't 'manage' very much, did you?
NICK	I never got a chance.
TONI	And whose fault is that? When you told me you'd booked a luxury hotel with double bed and *en suite* bathroom, I didn't expect to be sharing it with your best friend, your father-in-law, your sister-in-law and your wife! I could get you under the Trade Descriptions Act, I could. (*Knock.*) Come in!

(*Enter* CHRISTIAN.)

TONI	Hello, Christian.
HUGO	(*crossly*) What do you want?
CHRISTIAN	Well, sir –
HUGO	Go away.
TONI	Hugo!
CHRISTIAN	I was wondering, sir, if I might have a word with you in private.
HUGO	What the devil now?
CHRISTIAN	It is rather personal.
NICK	"Hotel and Catering", Hugo.
HUGO	Don't be silly. It's a survey.
CHRISTIAN	Is there somewhere we could go?
HUGO	I told you. I'm answering no more of your damned impertinent questions.
TONI	Don't give up, Christian.

HUGO	And you can mind your own business.
TONI	Go for it.
CHRISTIAN	Not the right moment, maybe. I'm sorry, sir. Good night.
HUGO	(*firmly*) Good night.

(*Exit* CHRISTIAN.)

NICK	You must attract them, Hugo.
TONI	No, it's not that.
NICK	Of course it's that. It's obvious. He's after a bit of 'how's your father'.
HUGO	How's your what?
NICK	Father.
TONI	That's funny.
NICK	It's an expression, Hugo.
TONI	He is. Sort of.
HUGO	What do you mean, 'an expression'?
NICK	(*irritated*) Never mind!
TONI	(*exploding*) Oh you two! I'm going to find somewhere to sleep. (*Pointedly, to* NICK.) On my own. Where's my bag? Oh yes . . .

(*She crosses to the closet and opens the door. Enter* SIR HARRY. TONI *screams in frustration.*)

SIR HARRY	Hello, girlie!
TONI	Ooh, you horrible old man! You're all slobbery and disgusting and I hate you! You ought to be thoroughly ashamed of yourselves, the lot of you. I'm going to bed.

(*Exit* TONI *to the adjoining room. She bolts the door.*)

SIR HARRY	Do you know something, Nick? I think you might be right about her. Girl must be a bloody Tasmanian.
HUGO	Tasmanian?
NICK	"Hotel and Catering" for women, Hugo.
SIR HARRY	Call it what you like. You can always spot 'em.
HUGO	Where am I going to sleep?
NICK	You can bunk up here, if you like.
HUGO	Here? Where?
NICK	Have a chair.
HUGO	I can't sleep in a chair.
NICK	You won't get a better offer. (*He gets into bed with* HILARY.)
HUGO	Oh all right. (*Yawning.*) I am very tired. (*He settles down for the night in one of the small armchairs.*)
NICK	(*firmly*) Goodnight. (*He soon falls asleep.*)
HILARY	(*in her sleep*) Good night.
SIR HARRY	Either of you fellows know what's happened to my blasted DJ?
HUGO	(*big yawn*) No idea.
SIR HARRY	I put it over this chair. Here.
HUGO	Ah. Then Christian must have taken it away. For cleaning.
SIR HARRY	I didn't ask for the confounded thing to be cleaned.
HUGO	You shouldn't have put it over the chair, then, should you? (*Little laugh, followed by another yawn.*)

SIR HARRY	Well, someone ring the boy up and tell him I want it back.
HUGO	Tell him yourself.
SIR HARRY	What?
HUGO	(*nearly asleep*) Just dial 9 and ask for Christian.
SIR HARRY	Humph! (*He crosses to the phone and dials.*) Hello?
HILARY	(*beginning to wake up*) Hello.
SIR HARRY	Hello? . . . Ah. Is that Christian?
HILARY	Daddy?
SIR HARRY	Where's my blasted dinner suit?
HILARY	Is that you?
SIR HARRY	Over the chair. Room 101.
HILARY	Where's Nick?
SIR HARRY	Then cancel it and bring it up.
HILARY	(*getting amorous*) Nicky!
SIR HARRY	Quick as you like. (*He puts the phone down.*)
HILARY	Nicky! Come on.
NICK	Not now, Hil, old chap.
HILARY	What are we doing with the lights on? You know I don't like it with the lights on. (*She turns off all the lights from a switch by the bed.*)
HUGO	(*in his sleep*) Good night.
SIR HARRY	What the hell's going on?
NICK	Hil. Darling . . . (HILARY *is getting very amorous.*) Aah! Not now. Please . . .
HILARY	But it's Saturday night.

NICK	Yes, darling. And I'm very tired.
HILARY	And it is the honeymoon suite.
NICK	I know. And I've got a headache.
SIR HARRY	Will someone turn on the bloody lights. (NICK *turns the lights back on.*)
HILARY	(*disappearing under the duvet*) Oh Nick . . .
SIR HARRY	Thank God for that. (*The phone rings. He answers it.*) Hello? Christian? . . . What do you mean, tomorrow morning? . . . Well, it's a complete disgrace. I shall report this to the General Manager. (*He slams down the receiver.*) Bloody servants! (*He picks it up again and dials 0.*) Hello? Reception? . . . I want a mobile phone . . . No I don't want a mobile phone, you fool, I want to speak to one . . . Of course I know the bloody number . . . Well, why didn't you say so in the first place, you idiot? (*He dials* GERALD'S *mobile number.*) Hello? Gerald? . . . Oh God, bloody machines . . . Yes, yes, yes. Bollocks, bollocks, bollocks . . . Ah. Gerald. It's me. I'm in 101. I want you to find me a DJ – tie, dress shirt and all the trimmings. Quick as you like. Be up here in five minutes whether you get this message or not. Over and out. (*He puts the receiver down. There is a snore from* HUGO.) Humph! (*He settles down in the other chair to wait. We hear* HILARY *getting amorous again under the duvet: "Naughty Nicky!". This time* NICK *embraces her in his sleep. Knock.*) That was quick.

(*Enter* CHRISTIAN.)

SIR HARRY	What the devil do you want?
CHRISTIAN	I need to speak to Mister – (*Loud snore from* HUGO.)
SIR HARRY	Well?
CHRISTIAN	I just came to clear away the coffee things.

SIR HARRY	(*closing the door*) Then don't just stand there, man. Get on with it.
CHRISTIAN	Yes, Lord Chancellor. (*Knock.*)
SIR HARRY	Answer that.
CHRISTIAN	Yes, Lord Chancellor.

(CHRISTIAN *opens the door. Enter* LIZ. CHRISTIAN *starts to clear away the coffee.*)

LIZ	Father?
SIR HARRY	What the blazes do you want?
LIZ	I came to see Nick.
SIR HARRY	He's in bed. Dead to the world.
LIZ	(*seeing them in bed*) With Hilary?
SIR HARRY	It's what married couples do, old thing.
LIZ	Thank goodness for that. What's Hugo doing here?
SIR HARRY	The girlie's thrown him out. Serve him right, the wimp. It was all a front anyway. Bloody Australian.
LIZ	You are such a stupid man! You know full well that Hugo isn't gay – as if it mattered anyway. (CHRISTIAN, *having finished clearing, is preparing to go. He stops and takes a keen interest in the following.*) You know that he and I were lovers when I was a pupil in Chambers.
SIR HARRY	Pah! You don't expect me to believe that a bit of puppy love all those years ago proves that Hugo's not – what do they call it? – "Home and Colonial".
LIZ	Don't be so ridiculous. (HILARY *wakes up and begins to take notice.*)
SIR HARRY	It's a statement of fact, Elizabeth.

LIZ	Hugo and I adored each other. We were going to get married.
SIR HARRY	I didn't invest all that money –
LIZ	Here we go again. You didn't invest all that money in my career so I could throw everything away on a penniless young barrister with no connections and no prospects. After all you'd done for me! The first woman in Chambers! Blah-blah-blah! Pity you didn't have a son to continue the Lumsden-Clark line, then you might have left us in peace. Hugo a wimp? Spectacular error of judgement, don't you think? He's Head of Chambers, in case you hadn't noticed, a leading and highly respected Q C, and everyone agrees he'd have been a High Court Judge long ago but for your misguided bigotry.
HILARY	Well said, sis.
SIR HARRY	(*to* HILARY) I didn't ask your opinion.
HILARY	You never ask anyone's opinion. That's half your trouble.
SIR HARRY	(*to* LIZ) After all I've done for you.
LIZ	I wish I'd never listened to you. (*She crosses to the door.*) You've ruined my life!
CHRISTIAN	Excuse me, miss...
	(*Exit* LIZ.)
CHRISTIAN	If I could just have a word...
	(*Exit* CHRISTIAN, *leaving the coffee.*)
SIR HARRY	Who rattled her cage?
HILARY	Do you mean to say you actually made her give Hugo up?
SIR HARRY	Hysterical exhibition.

HILARY	I'm serious. Did you?
SIR HARRY	Would never have worked, anyway.
HILARY	You were jealous of Hugo.
SIR HARRY	Don't be absurd. She had to choose. Marriage or career.
HILARY	Oh for God's sake.
SIR HARRY	She's a Circuit Judge, you know. At forty-four. Not bad.
HILARY	And that's all down to you, is it?
SIR HARRY	She couldn't have done it without me. (*Knock.*) Come!
GERALD	(*off*) It's Gerald, Lord Chancellor.
SIR HARRY	(*getting up to open the door*) Ah. Gerald.

(*Enter* GERALD *with* SIR HARRY'S *Act One suit, but with no shirt or tie*)

GERALD	Your dinner jacket, Lord Chancellor –
SIR HARRY	(*exploding*) That is not a dinner jacket!
GERALD	No, Lord Chancellor –
SIR HARRY	(*shouting*) Do you think I'm blind or something?

(TONI *bangs on the connecting door.* NICK *starts to wake up.*)

GERALD	What I'm trying to say, Lord Chancellor –
SIR HARRY	Spit it out, man.
GERALD	I couldn't find your dinner jacket.
SIR HARRY	Of course you couldn't, you imbecile. It's at the cleaners. I told you. (*More banging.*)

TONI	(*off, shouting*) Will you lot shut up in there!
GERALD	You didn't, Lord Chancellor.
SIR HARRY	Are you arguing with me?
GERALD	I'm sorry, Lord Chancellor, but I have a record of your message on my mobile telephone voice-mail service. If you would care for verification –
SIR HARRY	Just give me the suit and stop wittering. (*More banging.* SIR HARRY *starts putting his trousers on.*)
HILARY	(*to* NICK) What's going on next door?
NICK	No idea. Workmen, I expect. (*More banging.*)
TONI	(*off*) Some people around here are trying to get some sleep!
HILARY	Workmen?
NICK	Night shift. Probably.
SIR HARRY	(*increasingly angry*) Where's the bloody shirt? (*Sustained banging.*)
GERALD	You didn't ask for a shirt, Lord Chancellor.
SIR HARRY	Yes, I did. Tie, dress shirt and all the trimmings.
GERALD	I don't think you'd want to wear a dress shirt with this suit, Lord Chancellor. You'd risk looking very silly.
SIR HARRY	Right. That does it. You're fired.
GERALD	Fired, Lord Chancellor?
SIR HARRY	Sacked, you idiot!
GERALD	(*yelping with joy*) Wha-hey! (*He gives* SIR HARRY *a big kiss on the cheek.*)
SIR HARRY	What the devil –

(Enter TONI *from the adjoining room as* GERALD *slumps down in the spare chair in a state of relieved euphoria and pours himself a coffee.)*

TONI Will you lot just shut up!

HILARY Mm. Night shift, Nicholas?

NICK Er...

HILARY Night shift or nightie-shift, I wonder...

SIR HARRY Can't a man get dressed in peace without all these infernal interruptions?

(Enter LIZ, *rather more sober. She is followed by* CHRISTIAN.*)*

LIZ Father –

SIR HARRY Oh for God's sake. Now what do you want?

LIZ Be quiet, father, and listen. I have something very important that I want you to hear. It concerns Hugo.

SIR HARRY Pah!

(HUGO *begins to wake up during this story.*)

LIZ This is rather difficult... *(She braces herself.)* Shortly after I broke off my... relationship with Hugo I discovered that I was going to have a child. There was nobody I could turn to. It was too late to tell Hugo. So I went away and had the baby in secret. I gave my name as Elizabeth Smith for the purposes of the birth certificate. And I decided to have the child put up for adoption. When I came back I moved Chambers. I couldn't face the prospect of seeing Hugo every day and being reminded of everything I had lost. I pursued my career as best I could. I've always known that I betrayed Hugo, picking a stupid quarrel with him as a way of ending our relationship. And then hiding from him the knowledge of our son. But I felt the best way I

	could continue to express my love for him was to leave him free to build his own life.
HUGO	I have a son?
LIZ	Yes, Hugo.
HUGO	Why didn't you tell me? I have a son!
LIZ	I'm sorry, Hugo. What I did was wrong.
HUGO	Where is he now? My son.
CHRISTIAN	Here, father. I'm here.
HUGO	Christian?
CHRISTIAN	Father!
HUGO	You? Are you my son?
LIZ	It's true, Hugo. Christian is our son.
HUGO	My son! (HUGO *and* CHRISTIAN *embrace. Excitedly:*) Gerald, meet my son! Miss Taylor – my son! Christian, meet your Uncle Nick and your Auntie Hilary! Sir Harry – Christian! Your grandson!
SIR HARRY	Just a minute. Hold your horses. How do we know this is the real boy? He could be an imposter.
TONI	Go on, Christian. Show him your birth certificate.
	(CHRISTIAN *produces his birth certificate and hands it to* SIR HARRY.)
SIR HARRY	"Father: Unknown. Mother: Elizabeth Smith. Spinster". Good God.
HUGO	My son! I told you he was my son!
LIZ	Hugo. Can you ever forgive me?

SIR HARRY	Just leave everything to me, my son.
HUGO	But I'm not interested in your rotten patronage.
SIR HARRY	What?
HUGO	Do you seriously expect me to accept favours from you? You sexist, lecherous, bullying, hypocritical, old . . . fart!
GERALD	Wha-hey!
SIR HARRY	How dare you!
HUGO	Daring doesn't enter into it, you reactionary old dinosaur. I've always been in awe of you. Respected you. Looked up to you. How wrong I was. This weekend's been a revelation. I wouldn't have missed it for the world. Do you know what? You can stuff your judgeship. Besides, I've decided to take early retirement. To spend more time with my family.
LIZ	Oh Hugo!
CHRISTIAN	Good on you, Dad.
HUGO	Our son!
SIR HARRY	(*muscling in*) And my grandson, don't you forget that. Come here, Christian, and give the old dinosaur a hug. (CHRISTIAN *and* SIR HARRY *embrace warmly.*) At least now we know there are no bloody Australians in the family.
LIZ	(*wearily*) Father . . .
HILARY	(*warning*) Daddy . . .
CHRISTIAN	I shouldn't be so sure, Grandfather. (*He kisses* SIR HARRY.) I shouldn't be so sure!

(*"Waltzing Matilda" playout.*)

HUGO	There's nothing to forgive. I have everything I've ever wished for. I have a son. I have a family. Haven't I? (*Beat.*) Elizabeth?
LIZ	Oh Hugo. Do you mean . . . ? (*She moves to* HUGO *and they embrace.*)
HILARY	So, now we know who everybody is. Except Miss . . . Taylor, I think you said your name was?
TONI	Mmm.
HILARY	Hugo?
HUGO	She's nothing to do with me.
NICK	Hugo!
HILARY	(*steadily and with irony, mainly directed at* NICK) Oh I know who she must be, then, this attractive, seductive little secretary, running around our hotel bedroom in her underwear. She must be one of Daddy's girls. Don't you think so, Nicholas? Just as well you're a widower, Daddy, because if Mummy were here she might be just a teeny weeny bit cross. (*Increasingly focused on* NICK.) He did try it once, you know, but he wasn't very clever and Mummy found out and told Daddy that if it ever happened again, Mummy would divorce him. On the spot. And he never dared try it again. (NICK, *along with everybody else, has understood the message.*)
SIR HARRY	So, Hugo. I understand you're interested in becoming a High Court Judge.
LIZ	(*appalled*) Father!
SIR HARRY	We could do with more red-blooded Englishmen on the Bench.
HILARY	(*appalled*) Daddy!
SIR HARRY	Nothing wrong with Hugo. I can see that now.
HUGO	Thank you, Sir Harry –